The Psalms
in Common Meter

by D. Scott Foote

I0155721

Copyright © 2013, 2020, by D. Scott Foote

Second Edition

Versions of the Psalms found in *The Psalms in Common Meter* may be reproduced in any form without express permission of the author provided: the quotations occur in non-salable media; no more than five Psalms are quoted at any time; and appropriate acknowledgment is given. Requests for commercial use (or for more extensive quotation) should be addressed to the author at:

psaltercm@gmail.com

All other rights reserved.

Cover photo of Lake Michigan taken July 27, 2019 near Spring Lake, Michigan.

Printed in the United States of America
Published by Braughler Books LLC., Springboro, Ohio

ISBN: 978-1-970063-69-1

Library of Congress Control Number: 2014951393

Ordering information: Special discounts are available on quantity purchases by bookstores, corporations, associations, and others. For details, contact the publisher at:

sales@braughlerbooks.com
or at 937-58-BOOKS

For questions or comments about this book, please write to:

psaltercm@gmail.com

Braughler™
Books
braughlerbooks.com

Preface

When the first edition of *The Psalms In Common Meter* was published seven years ago, it was a time of relative stability in our country. How different it is today in 2020 as we are confronted by a global pandemic, financial implosion, and racial protests. Never before have we faced simultaneous business and school closures, job layoffs, stay-at-home orders, and social unrest. No one is immune, and many of us are shaken, fearful, and angry. We are desperate for healing and restoration, though this feels like a distant hope at best. To paraphrase Thomas Paine, these are times that try our souls.

In times such as these, God's people have always returned to the Psalms – the great soul book of the Bible. The Psalms give voice to what we are experiencing and feeling. When we pray the Psalms we are joining our voice to those of countless others through the ages. *The Psalms in Common Meter* is a unique expression of that voice. This can be an easy on-ramp for those new to the Psalter, as well as a fresh look at these ancient poems for those longer in the faith.

The emotions of the Psalms are real and they are raw. Whatever we are feeling, there is almost certainly a Psalm that expresses it. When we are overwhelmed by fear, anger, or despair, there are Psalms of Lament. When we are in need of hope, there are Psalms of Trust. And when we are filled with gratitude, there are Psalms of Worship.

Psalms of Lament give voice to our suffering as we cry out to God.

- *"For I am faint and feeble, Lord, my body aches and groans; O heal me from my maladies and pain within my bones." (Psalm 6:2)*

- *"My heart despairs from anguishing, it's paralyzed by fright; I'm terrorized by thoughts of death that plague me in the night. Concerns and troubles panic me for fear is in control; the horror that consumes my mind has overwhelmed my soul." (Psalm 55:4-5)*

- *"How long, O Lord, will evil reign? How long will it prevail? How long until the wicked fall? How long until they fail?" (Psalm 94:3)*

Psalms of Trust give voice to our hope as we place our faith in God.

- *"Our God's a refuge and our strength and always at our side, a timely help when trouble comes, an ever-present guide. Although the earth erupts in quakes, we will not shake or fear; though glaciers crash into the sea, our God is always near." (Psalm 46:1-2)*

- *"My soul finds rest in God alone because of grace He shows; my hope and rescue come from Him, for I'm the one He chose." (Psalm 62:1)*

- *"Just like a bird protects its young beneath its outstretched wing, God's faithfulness will be your shield, a rock on which to cling. And you will never know the grip of terror in the night,*

*or any arrow flying high upon the morning
light. Nor will there be a pestilence to dread
when day is gone, or any epidemic scourge to
fear when comes the dawn." (Psalm 91:4-6)*

Psalms of Praise give voice to our worship as
we express our gratitude to God.

- *"O Lord, our Lord, how wonderful Your name
  in all the earth; the splendor of the heavens
  shows Your glory and Your worth."
  (Psalm 8:1)*

- *"My heart is ever true, O God, my heart is
  ever true; my lips will sing the sweetest song
  to praise and worship You. Awake my soul,
  arise with me, awake O harp and strings;
  together we will wake the dawn as all creation
  sings. And I will worship You, O Lord, and
  thank You all my days; among the people
  everywhere, I'll ever sing Your praise. For
  greater is Your faithfulness than sun and stars
  above; and higher still than heaven's throne is
  Your unfailing love." (Psalm 57:7-10)*

- *"O sing unto the Lord a song, a new song let us
  sing; let all the earth join in this song and let
  His praises ring. O sing unto the Lord a song,
  a song that gives Him praise; so His salvation
  is proclaimed today and all our days. Tell
  nations He is glorious, magnificent and grand;
  proclaim the wonders of His acts to people in
  the land." (Psalm 96:1-3)*

The Psalms have endured for over 3000 years precisely because they are God's Word authentically speaking to the universal needs of the soul. For these millennia they have been a strong tower of righteousness against the arrows of evil; a river of joy against the shores of despair; a healing balm against the open sores of fear; and a song of praise against the emptiness of idolatry. May they be that for you and more.

S

Preface to the First Edition

My first exposure to a metrical psalter came on a chilly winter's evening in 2005 during a worship service of the Free Church of Scotland held in Xenia, Ohio. We gathered in a small rural Friends meetinghouse as a group of perhaps a dozen or so worshippers. I can still remember rising from the hard wooden pew when a lone congregant started to sing (a cappella) a metered Psalm. The rest of us enthusiastically joined in as we raised our voices praising God – no instruments, no electronics, *sola scriptura*. This thoroughly delightful experience was enhanced by the knowledge that we were following a form of worship essentially unchanged for centuries. The version of the Psalms used that evening came from *"The Scottish Metrical Psalter,"* which was approved by the Church of Scotland in 1650 to be used in public worship. To hear these songs of praise to God from a centuries-old version of the Psalms was a spiritual moment indeed – the kingdom of God breaking through in the simplicity and mysterious beauty of His Word. It was during this service that the seed of creating a metrical version of the Psalms in contemporary language was planted in my heart.

Metered versions of the Psalms go back at least to the Protestant Reformation where many Christians saw Holy Scripture, and particularly the Psalms, as the preferred if not exclusive form of worship text. Over the years there have been scores if not hundreds of metered translations of the Psalms in English, French, German, and other languages. In fact, many of the earliest printed Bibles included a separate metrical psalter. Of course, the Psalms in their original Hebrew are poetry, although of a form based more on imagery, concentration of ideas, and parallelism than the standard measures and rhyming that are the essence of meter. While entire Psalms in metered form are largely out of favor in our day, many metered verses live on in contemporary worship songs.

My goal in this translation is to provide a rhythmic version of the Psalms in an easily understood and hopefully enjoyable form. The decision to use common meter in a verse-by-verse translation was arbitrary. However, common meter rests gently on the ear, and is a metrical form familiar to churchgoers in many of the great hymns of the faith such as *Amazing Grace, O God Our Help In Ages Past,* and *All Hail The Power Of Jesus' Name."* The choice of a specific meter imposes a nonnegotiable in the translation, which therefore necessitates license in interpretation of individual verses. Beyond the constraint of metrical form, I have done my utmost to be faithful to the meaning of the text – applying principles of dynamic equivalence while retaining original structure as much as possible. The intent is to make each Psalm clear without losing the flavor of the more familiar and cherished verses.

Metrical Psalms are to be sung or read aloud, thus my choice of words and sentence structure has favored the spoken word. I have endeavored to have the verses flow together and to make the relationships between verses clear and sensible. I have also sought to clarify the antecedent basis of pronouns where there is ambiguity. Many Psalms also switch liberally between first, second and third person, which no doubt has a poetic purpose in the original Hebrew. Even in English translations this can have a dramatic effect, such as in Psalm 23 where the psalmist David switches from the third person to the second person in verse four. However, in other instances it can be distracting to the flow. Thus, I have attempted to use the same point of view (or at least reduce the number of transitions) throughout a given Psalm.

I am grateful to Amy Monahan-Curtis for her editorial assistance. She has a wonderful understanding of language and provided invaluable guidance into meaning, structure and word choice.

Finally, to my wife Pat – thank you for so patiently reviewing this work and your numerous suggestions to keep me faithful to the text. You have been a constant source of encouragement and inspiration. You are an amazing woman of God and I am truly blessed to have your love.

S - June, 2013

Psalm 1

1 How happy those who do not stray
  to where the wicked walk,
Or stand with sinners on their way,
  or sit with those who mock.

2 But those who love the law of God
  have found their hearts' delight;
And on His word they meditate
  all day and through the night.

3 They flourish like a tree that's near
  a river flowing by,
Which bears its fruit all season long,
  with leaves that never die.

4 Not so the wicked and the vile
  who do not thrive or grow;
For they are scattered like the chaff
  when winds begin to blow.

5 And thus the wicked will not know
  the joy and great reward,
Of being with the pure in heart
  and those who love the Lord.

6 For He will watch and guard the just,
  the righteous He'll defend;
Not so the wicked who will fall
  and perish in the end.

Psalm 2

1 Why do the people seethe and shout?
  Why are they so enraged?
Why do they plot conspiracies?
  Why are they thus engaged?

2 Their kings revolt against the Lord
    and what His hand has done;
Their leaders plot against His king,
    the Lord's anointed one.

3 They say, *"We do not like their rule,*
    we need to break away;
Let's free ourselves from their constraints,
    from all control and sway."

4 The Lord looks down from heaven's realm
    at rebels in the lands;
He laughs to see their feeble plots
    and mocks them for their plans.

5 But then He rises in His rage,
    no longer does He laugh;
With anger born of righteousness,
    He pours on them His wrath.

6 The Lord declares, *"O hear my voice,*
    and listen to my will;
In Zion I've installed my king
    upon my holy hill."

7 The Lord announces to the king,
    "Today, You are my son;
I've chosen and appointed You
    as my anointed one.

8 *Just ask the things you want from me —*
    the nations and the earth;
I'll make them your inheritance,
    a treasure of great worth.

9 *Exert your will upon their lives,*
    and rule with iron hand;
Or shatter them like pottery,
    whatever you command."

¹⁰ So every rebel be forewarned
    and listen to this voice;
Be wise, take heed, and rightly judge,
    for you can make this choice –

¹¹ To serve the Lord with reverence,
    with homage bowing low,
And worship Him most joyfully
    as honor you bestow.

¹² O be respectful to the king
    so you are not destroyed;
But take your refuge in the Lord,
    and you'll be overjoyed.

Psalm 3

¹ O Lord, I cannot stop to count
    the number of my foes;
They rise and come against me now
    and strike me with their blows.

² Their jeering voices shout at me
    as mockingly they say,
"His God will not protect his life,
    He will not make a way."

³ But Lord, You are my strength and shield,
    You will not pass me by;
You honor me with victory
    and lift my head up high.

⁴ For when I cry to You for help,
    You listen to my plea;
From high upon Your holy hill,
    Your answer comes to me.

⁵ When I lie down to rest at night
    to gently find my sleep,
I know that when the morning dawns
    I'll wake within Your keep.

⁶ I will not fear a thousand swords
    drawn up on every side,
  Nor tens of thousands threatening
    from places far and wide.

⁷ Arise, my God, deliver me,
    and keep my foes at bay;
  Strike every mouth and shatter teeth
    and save me from the fray.

⁸ O Lord, from You salvation comes,
    in You the weary rest;
  From You comes true deliverance
    so faithful souls are blessed.

Psalm 4

¹ O God, please answer when I pray
    and listen to my plea;
  Relieve me for I'm in distress,
    O pour Your grace on me.

² How long, O fools, will you attempt
    to make my shame complete?
  How long will you pursue what's false
    and practice your deceit?

³ Beware and know the Lord has claimed
    the righteous for His own;
  He hears me when I call to Him
    amid each cry and groan.

⁴ So though you tremble and you rage,
    in anger do not sin;
  But meditate and search your heart
    and thoughts that dwell within.

⁵ And give to God a sacrifice
    by doing what is right;
  Put confidence and trust in Him
    by walking in His light.

⁶ O Lord, so many tongues cry out
    for blessings every day;
  They ask that You would show Your face
    to shine and guide their way.

⁷ But You give me a greater joy
    than stores of wine and grain;
  A joy much sweeter than the breeze
    that comes behind the rain.

⁸ For I am filled with peacefulness
    when lying down to sleep;
  With You, O Lord, I rest secure
    and safe within Your keep.

Psalm 5

¹ O Lord, please hear these words of mine,
    consider every sigh;
  Be present and attend to me
    and do not pass me by.

² Please listen to my cries for help
    to You my God and King;
  Do not ignore or disregard
    these anguished prayers I bring.

³ I ask that when the morning dawns
    that You will hear my plea,
  In hopeful expectation, Lord,
    that You will answer me.

⁴ Where there is hate, You take no joy,
    where evil, no delight;
  For no one who is bad or vile
    will dwell within Your sight.

⁵ You hate the proud and arrogant,
    You loathe the things they do;
  They cannot stand when You are near,
    they find no help from You.

⁶ You can't abide a perjurer
　　or those who seek to kill;
You crush them for their wicked acts
　　and guiltless blood they spill.

⁷ But I have come into Your house
　　through Your redeeming grace,
And bow to You in reverence
　　within that holy place.

⁸ Because I have so many foes,
　　reveal to me Your way;
And lead me in Your righteousness
　　to do Your will each day.

⁹ My enemies have wicked hearts
　　that fill me with disgust;
Their throats are like an open grave
　　with words I cannot trust.

¹⁰ Declare their guilt both far and wide
　　so all their sins are known;
And banish them as punishment
　　like one would toss a stone.

¹¹ But honor those who love Your name
　　and praise You with their voice;
Protect those who delight in You
　　and in Your care rejoice.

¹² O Lord, You bless the good and just,
　　You fill them with Your love;
You keep them safe from enemies
　　and guard them from above.

Psalm 6

¹ O Lord, do not admonish me
　　or let Your anger burn;
Withhold Your hand of discipline,
　　and do not be so stern.

² For I am faint and feeble, Lord,
 my body aches and groans;
O heal me from my maladies
 and pain within my bones.

³ My soul is weak from suffering,
 so tell me, Lord, how long –
How long must I await relief
 till once again I'm strong?

⁴ Lord, turn Your head and look at me,
 deliver me today;
O save me by Your endless grace,
 come now without delay.

⁵ For lips can't thank You from the grave,
 no words are heard from there;
The dead will never sing Your praise
 or come to You in prayer.

⁶ My strength is sapped from suffering
 and sobs that flood my bed;
I have no way to stem the flow
 or stop the tears I shed.

⁷ My eyes are growing weak and dim
 with sorrow from my plight,
Because of all my enemies
 who threaten day and night.

⁸ I shout at those surrounding me
 to turn around and flee;
The vile should listen and beware
 since God has heard my plea.

⁹ For they will know that when I cry,
 the Lord reveals His care;
He listens to what I request
 and answers every prayer.

10 My enemies will be dismayed
　　and shamed by their defeat;
　Dishonored and in disarray,
　　they'll suddenly retreat.

Psalm 7

1 O Lord my God, I find my help
　　and hideaway in You;
　So rescue and deliver me
　　from people who pursue.

2 For like a lion on the hunt,
　　they'll rip me with their claws,
　Then drag me where I can't be saved
　　to crush me in their jaws.

3 O Lord, if I am culpable,
　　if I have unclean hands,
　If I have acted wickedly
　　or made unfair demands –

4 If I have wrongly hurt a friend
　　or broken any peace,
　If I have robbed my enemies
　　or ruled them by caprice –

5 Then let them overtake me, Lord,
　　for surely this is just;
　And let them cut and trample me
　　and leave me in the dust.

6 But come now, Lord, and be my judge,
　　in righteous anger stand;
　Condemn my foes by giving them
　　the justice You demand.

7 Bid every nation far and wide
　　to come and gather nigh;
　Prepare a verdict for their deeds,
　　a ruling from on high.

⁸ And since You judge the people, Lord,
    I ask that You judge me,
According to my righteousness
    and actions that You see.

⁹ O righteous everlasting God,
    Who knows each mind and heart,
Cut off the scourge of wickedness
    and set our lives apart.

¹⁰ My God protects and watches me
    and covers like a shield;
He saves the just and pure of heart
    and all whose spirits yield.

¹¹ His righteous judgments are correct
    and always on display;
He pours His wrath upon the vile
    and wicked every day.

¹² For God will bend and train His bow
    at those who don't repent;
His arm will swing His two-edged sword
    unless their hearts relent.

¹³ He's holding arrows in His hand,
    their tips alight with flame;
Like shooting stars across the night,
    He's making sure their aim.

¹⁴ The wicked think of evil thoughts
    with hatred in their eyes;
They stir up trouble with their deeds
    then cover them with lies.

¹⁵ Yet anyone who digs a hole
    in soft and shifting sand,
Will fall into the pit they made
    without a saving hand.

¹⁶ For all the evil that they sow
  is what their lives will reap;
And all their violence in the end
  will make them mourn and weep.

¹⁷ So I will thank and bless the Lord
  for righteous are His ways;
I'll sing unto the Lord Most High
  and lift His name in praise.

Psalm 8

¹ O Lord, our Lord, how wonderful
  Your name in all the earth;
The splendor of the heavens shows
  Your glory and Your worth.

² The mouths of babes and children sing
  to You the sweetest praise;
They silence all Your enemies
  with every song they raise.

³ O when I contemplate the sky
  with moon and stars above,
I think about Your awesome works
  created by Your love.

⁴ Compared to all these marvels, Lord,
  I wonder why You care,
For humans walking on the earth –
  mere mortals breathing air.

⁵ You made us lower than Yourself
  yet gave each one a crown –
Of honor and of dignity
  and glory of renown.

⁶ You made us ruler of the works
  created by Your hands –
All creatures moving here and there
  in waters and the lands;

7 The flocks of sheep and herds of cows
    that graze in every field;
The animals that we can tame
    and those that will not yield;

8 The birds that soar above the earth
    and fish that swim below;
In skies above or oceans deep,
    no matter where they go.

9 O Lord, our Lord, how wonderful
    Your name in all the earth;
The name above all other names,
    the name of greatest worth.

Psalm 9

1 O Lord, I give my thanks to You
    and praise Your holy name;
With all my heart, Your mighty works
    and wonders I proclaim.

2 I overflow with gladness, Lord,
    rejoicing in Your ways;
I worship and delight in You
    and ever sing Your praise.

3 My foes turn back when You appear
    because their lives are through;
They stumble as they try to run,
    then die in front of You.

4 O Lord, You've judged with righteousness
    while seated on Your throne;
You've heard my plea and weighed my cause
    and justice to me shown.

5 The wayward nations You condemn,
    the wicked You abhor;
Their names are ever blotted out,
    remembered nevermore.

⁶ My enemies have met their end,
    their reign of evil done;
You've wiped their cities from the earth,
    forgotten everyone.

⁷ The Lord is King from age to age,
    forevermore He reigns;
And from His throne the world will hear
    the judgments He proclaims.

⁸ The Lord will rule in righteousness
    all people everywhere;
With justice He will govern them,
    His verdicts always fair.

⁹ The Lord will be a hideaway
    for those who are oppressed,
A mighty fort in troubled times,
    a place of peace and rest.

¹⁰ The Lord will never turn His back
    on those who trust in Him;
His care for them will never fade,
    nor His compassion dim.

¹¹ The Lord God reigns from Zion's hill
    so let us sing His praise,
And tell the nations of His deeds
    and marvels of His ways.

¹² The Lord remembers those in pain,
    their cries are in His mind;
He punishes their enemies,
    repaying them in kind.

¹³ O Lord, please see my suffering
    when enemies assail;
Be merciful and rescue me
    so death does not prevail.

¹⁴ Then in Jerusalem I'll sing
    and worship You with praise;
I'll tell of Your salvation, Lord,
    and how You've blessed my days.

¹⁵ The nations have been hoisted high
    upon their own petard;
They snag their feet in snares they laid,
    they trip and fall down hard.

¹⁶ The Lord is known for righteousness
    as shown by His commands;
He traps the wicked in the nets
    they set with their own hands.

¹⁷ The vile are destined for the grave,
    there will not be a stay;
For all who turn away from God
    will surely pass away.

¹⁸ The Lord will not forget the poor,
    He knows each broken heart;
Where there is need, He offers hope
    that never will depart.

¹⁹ Arise, O Lord, against my foes
    so none of them prevails;
Judge all of them in front of You,
    and weigh them on Your scales.

²⁰ Lord, strike the wicked for their deeds
    and fill their hearts with fear;
O show them their mortality –
    that death will soon appear.

Psalm 10

¹ O Lord, why do You stay away?
    Why do You not appear?
Why do You seem to hide Yourself
    when trouble is so near?

² The wicked show their arrogance
  as scornfully they seek,
To persecute the destitute
  and trap the poor and weak.

³ The wicked boast of fame and wealth
  and cravings deep within,
Affirming greed, and hating God
  in unremorseful sin.

⁴ The wicked do not look for God,
  their eyes for Him are blind;
They do not care about the Lord
  or keep His ways in mind.

⁵ The wicked seem so prosperous,
  with no concerns or woes;
They do not seek to know God's laws,
  they sneer at all their foes.

⁶ The wicked say about themselves,
  "O we will thrive and grow;
Our happiness will never end,
  no trouble will we know."

⁷ The wicked spew an endless stream
  of curses, lies, and threats;
Their tongues reveal their evil hearts,
  which never have regrets.

⁸ The wicked lurk near villages,
  in shadows deep and dark;
With vicious minds they seek to kill
  an unsuspecting mark.

⁹ They stalk like lions on a hunt
  and watch for easy prey;
They catch their quarries in a trap
  then drag them far away.

¹⁰ The wicked strike their victims hard
    to knock and beat them down;
They overwhelm them by their strength
    and crush them in the ground.

¹¹ The wicked think that God is blind,
    and say, *"He does not see;*
The Lord has covered up His face
    and does not notice me."

¹² Arise, O Lord, and hear the cry
    of those afflicted so;
Lift up Your hand to help the weak
    and helpless here below.

¹³ Why do the wicked treat You, Lord,
    with hatred and contempt?
Why do they think that You will let
    their actions be exempt?

¹⁴ For you, O God, see those in tears
    with grief upon their face;
The victim's soul is in Your care,
    within Your close embrace.

¹⁵ So crush the wicked for their wrongs
    and evil of their ways;
And punish those with sinful hearts
    by cutting short their days.

¹⁶ O Lord, You are the timeless King
    Who evermore will reign;
Though nations ebb and disappear,
    You always will remain.

¹⁷ You hear the lowly when they pray,
    You don't ignore their cries;
You lift them and encourage them
    to make their spirits rise.

¹⁸ O Lord, with You the poor are safe
    and orphans are secure;
  Through You the scourge of wickedness
    and terror is no more.

Psalm 11

¹ In God alone I put my trust
    so don't exclaim to me,
  "Escape to mountains far away,
    take wing and swiftly flee."

² Don't shout, *"The wicked bend their bows*
    and draw their strings up tight;
  They aim to shoot their arrows straight
    at those whose hearts are right."

³ And don't declare, *"Our lives are doomed*
    for things are falling down –
  What can the righteous hope to do
    with chaos all around?"

⁴ The Lord has not forsaken us,
    He watches from His throne;
  For Him there's nothing people do
    that's hidden or unknown.

⁵ The Lord looks at the good and just
    whose hearts are pure and right;
  He hates the wicked and the vile
    whose souls are dark as night.

⁶ His justice burns on wickedness
    like fire flamed by wind,
  That sears the lungs and blinds the eyes
    and chars and blisters skin.

⁷ The Lord is filled with righteousness,
    His justice shows His grace;
  The upright come to know His love
    and gaze upon His face.

Psalm 12

[1] O Lord, where have the godly gone?
     When did they go away?
   Why did the faithful disappear?
     Where do they dwell today?

[2] For everyone obscures the truth,
     their speech is full of lies,
   Their flattery a covering,
     their words a dark disguise.

[3] O Lord, repay the arrogant
     and those who falsely praise;
   O silence wagging tongues that boast,
     and end their bragging ways.

[4] The proud are trusting in their lips
     to get the things they need;
   They hope the clever words they speak
     will make their plans succeed.

[5] O Lord, You comfort those who groan
     and care for the maligned;
   You rise to save the poor and weak
     from those who are unkind.

[6] Your words are like the silver ore
     that furnace heat refines,
   By purifying sevenfold
     until it brightly shines.

[7] O Lord, You watch and shelter us
     from those who've gone astray;
   You save us from the evilness
     that's near us every day.

[8] For everywhere the wicked go
     they strut around and smile,
   Because the world is filled with hate
     and honors what is vile.

Psalm 13

1 How long will You forget me, Lord,
  and disregard my plea?
How long will You conceal Yourself
  and hide Your face from me?

2 How long will troubles plague my mind
  and sorrows fill my heart?
How long until my foes are stopped
  and enemies depart?

3 O Lord, my God, please answer me
  and let me see Your light;
Restore my strength and give me hope,
  or death will be my plight.

4 Don't let my adversaries gloat
  and talk of how they've won;
Don't let them celebrate my fall
  by thinking I am done.

5 O Lord, I always put my trust
  in Your unfailing love;
My heart delights because You save
  and lift me from above.

6 My lips will ever give You thanks
  by singing songs of praise;
For You are kind and caring, Lord,
  with goodness all my days.

Psalm 14

1 The foolish speak from reckless hearts,
  "There is no God," they say;
With actions vile and fraudulent,
  they all have gone astray.

² The Lord is looking from His throne
    to see if He can find,
If anyone is seeking Him
    with all their heart and mind.

³ But all have turned from righteousness,
    corruption they extol;
There's no one who is doing good,
    no, not a single soul.

⁴ Why have the wicked never learned
    to seek the Lord each day,
But rather feed on those who do
    like lions eat their prey?

⁵ The wicked will be terrified
    and overwhelmed with fear,
Because the Lord upholds the just,
    remaining ever near.

⁶ And though the wicked thwart the plans
    of those who are oppressed,
The Lord protects the innocent,
    and gives them peace and rest.

⁷ From Zion's hill salvation comes,
    let Israel rejoice;
And when the Lord makes captives whole,
    let Jacob raise his voice.

Psalm 15

¹ Lord, who may see Your sacred tent
    and find their rest inside,
Or live upon Your holy hill,
    and there with You abide?

² The ones who walk in righteousness
    and from it won't depart;
Who always have a word of truth
    and speak it from the heart.

³ They never slander or malign
  or treat a neighbor wrong;
They never criticize a friend
  but strive to get along.

⁴ They hate the vile, but honor those
  who trust and keep God's word;
They never break a promise made
  despite the cost incurred.

⁵ They never charge to make a loan,
  nor any bribe procure;
For those who do these things will thrive
  and always be secure.

Psalm 16

¹ O God, defend and keep me safe,
  protected and secure;
For I have always trusted You
  to make my refuge sure.

² I tell You truly, *"You're my Lord,*
  the source of everything;
You give me all that's pure and good,
  there's nothing that I bring."

³ As for the saints who walk the earth,
  I thank You, Lord, for them;
They fill me with delight and joy,
  each one a sparkling gem.

⁴ But those who follow other gods
  will suffer pain untold;
I'll not bow down or speak the names
  of idols they uphold.

⁵ O Lord, You give me all I need
  and everything I want;
You make me heir to all You own –
  a never-ending font.

⁶ How pleasant are the boundaries
    that You have set for me;
How lovely is the heritage,
    like years of jubilee.

⁷ I'll bless You when the morning dawns,
    I'll praise You in the night;
I'll listen to Your counsel, Lord,
    that sets my spirit right.

⁸ The thought of You is in my mind,
    it's You I long to see;
I'll not be shaken or be moved
    when You are close to me.

⁹ My heart is filled with peace and joy
    because of how it's blessed;
My soul has found security
    with hopefulness and rest.

¹⁰ For You will not abandon me
    or let me pass away;
You will not let Your Holy One
    experience decay.

¹¹ O Lord, You guide me on a path
    that offers life anew;
You fill me with eternal joy
    because I'm near to You.

Psalm 17

¹ O hear my plea for justice, Lord,
    and listen to my cry;
Attend to prayers I lift to You
    from lips that do not lie.

² For You will find me innocent
    and guiltless in Your sight;
Because You know what's fair and true
    and always judge what's right.

³ And though You search my heart at night
    and test it to be sure,
  No sinful thoughts are in my mind,
    no words I speak impure.

⁴ I know the wicked and their deeds,
    the evil things they do;
  I keep myself from violence,
    remaining close to You.

⁵ I walk along Your narrow path,
    I do not slip or stray;
  My feet have never lost their grip
    while following Your way.

⁶ O God, I call, and You respond
    because You always care;
  So turn Your head and hear these words,
    O listen to my prayer.

⁷ Lord, show the marvels of Your love,
    protect me by Your might;
  For I am saved by Your right hand
    from foes who want to fight.

⁸ O hold and keep me ever close,
    the apple of your eye;
  And hide me underneath Your wings,
    protected from on high.

⁹ And guard me from assailants, Lord,
    my many deadly foes,
  Who hem me in on every side
    to magnify my woes.

¹⁰ Their hearts are cold and motionless,
    no feelings stir inside;
  Their words reveal their hidden thoughts
    of arrogance and pride.

¹¹ The wicked follow after me
 wherever I am found,
Alertly watching for their chance
 to throw me to the ground.

¹² They stalk like lions on the hunt
 that hunger for their prey;
They linger in their hiding place
 until I come their way.

¹³ Arise, O Lord, confront my foes,
 it's time for them to fall;
And by Your sword deliver me
 from sinners one and all.

¹⁴ O save me, Lord, from such as these,
 who love their own affairs;
For their reward is in this life
 and what they leave their heirs.

¹⁵ But I will walk in righteousness
 and gaze upon Your face;
And waking to the rising sun,
 I'll revel in Your grace.

Psalm 18

¹ I love you Lord, You give me strength,
 You help me when I call;
You make me strong when I am weak,
 You catch me when I fall.

² The Lord is my deliverer,
 a refuge and a rock;
He saves me by His mighty hand,
 He answers when I knock.

³ And when I call upon the Lord
 and lift His name in praise,
I need not fear my enemies
 because the Lord God saves.

⁴ For once the fear of death entwined
   and trapped me in its web;
Entangled by its many cords,
   my strength began to ebb.

⁵ The fear of hell surrounded me
   and bound me like a rope;
The snares of death encircled me
   and cut off any hope.

⁶ In my distress, I cried to God
   to listen to my plea;
He heard me in His temple courts
   and turned His ears to me.

⁷ Then all the earth convulsed and shook,
   the mountains quaked and roared;
The hills were shaken by the wrath
   and anger of the Lord.

⁸ A cloud of smoke poured from His nose
   and fire from His head;
While flames erupted from His mouth
   that scorched the land He tread.

⁹ He split the heavens by His hand
   as down to earth He came;
With stormy clouds beneath His feet,
   His wrath was not restrained.

¹⁰ He rode on backs of cherubim
   whose flight was sure and fair;
He sped upon the wings of wind
   while soaring through air.

¹¹ And darkness was His hiding place
   that covered like a shroud;
A heavy fog enveloped Him,
   concealing like a cloud.

¹² In front of His bright shining light,
    thick waves of smoke were blown;
With wind and hail and lightning bolts,
    He made His presence known.

¹³ From heaven He projected out
    a thundering refrain,
Like hailstones echoing the beat
    of sleet and freezing rain.

¹⁴ He shot His arrows far and wide
    and scattered all my foes;
With flashing bolts and lightning strikes,
    He multiplied their woes.

¹⁵ The Lord revealed the hidden things
    by power of His breath,
From solid rock beneath the land
    to deepest ocean depth.

¹⁶ Then from above He lifted me
    from waters running deep;
He stretched His hand and picked me up
    and held me in His keep.

¹⁷ He shielded and protected me
    from every enemy,
From those who hate and loathe my life
    and those too strong for me.

¹⁸ Although my adversaries struck
    and beat me to the ground,
The Lord was my support and stay,
    a pillar firm and sound.

¹⁹ He brought me to a place of hope,
    of spaciousness and light;
And in His joy He rescued me
    because my heart was right.

20 He judges by the deeds I've done
    and righteousness He's seen;
The Lord rewards and blesses me
    because my hands are clean.

21 For I have always kept the ways
    the Lord our God has made;
I have not acted wickedly
    nor turned from Him and strayed.

22 I always follow His decrees,
    I keep them in my heart;
I will not wander from His path
    nor from His law depart.

23 Before the Lord I'm scrupulous,
    avoiding every wrong;
I've kept myself from sinful ways,
    remaining ever strong.

24 He blesses me for righteousness
    and following His ways;
He honors me for what I do
    and how I live my days.

25 O Lord, to every faithful soul,
    Your faithfulness is known;
And to the righteous and the pure,
    Your righteousness is shown.

26 And to the pure in mind and heart,
    Your pureness is displayed;
But to the crooked and the shrewd,
    Your wrath will not be stayed.

27 You save the humble and the meek
    when they are beaten down,
But humble those whose haughty eyes
    take pride in their renown.

²⁸ For You, O Lord, preserve my lamp
    and keep it burning bright;
For like the dawning of the day,
    You make my darkness light.

²⁹ With You beside me I am strong
    to challenge one and all,
To overcome all obstacles,
    to scale the highest wall.

³⁰ For You are good, Your way is right,
    Your word is true and pure;
You shield those trusting in Your name
    and make their lives secure.

³¹ For You, O Lord, are God alone,
    there's no one else like You;
You stand as our defense and shield,
    the Rock that sees us through.

³² O it is You who blesses me
    with strength for each new day,
Who guides me on a level path
    so perfect is my way.

³³ You make me agile like a deer
    that's nimble, lithe and spry;
You set me on a mountaintop
    that reaches to the sky.

³⁴ You train my hands to fight a war
    and battle every foe;
You strengthen me and build my arms
    so I can bend a bow.

³⁵ You keep me safe by shielding me,
    You make my pathway straight;
You hold Your right hand under me
    and stoop to make me great.

³⁶ You clear the path beneath my feet
from traps designed to trip,
So I can make my way along
without a turn or slip.

³⁷ I hunted and pursued my foes
to catch them as they fled;
I did not interrupt the chase
till all of them lay dead.

³⁸ I shattered and I crushed their lives
despite their many cries;
They tumbled down beneath my feet,
too broken to arise.

³⁹ You strengthened me for battle, Lord,
You armed me for the fight;
You routed every enemy
and put my foe to flight.

⁴⁰ You pushed my adversaries back,
You made them turn and flee;
You beat them on the battlefield
and won the victory.

⁴¹ They cried that You would rescue them,
their voices raised as one;
But when You did not answer them,
they knew that they were done.

⁴² I beat them down into the dust
that winds blow far away;
I trampled them into the roads
and left them to decay.

⁴³ O Lord, You saved me from attacks
to keep me from despair;
You made me king to rule my foes
and nations everywhere.

[44] As soon as any hear my voice,
   they follow and obey;
   While foreigners and strangers too
   submit without delay.

[45] For all of them are terrified,
   they tremble in their fear;
   They stumble from their hideaways
   whenever I am near.

[46] O Lord, You live!   So let the earth
   lift up Your name in praise;
   Exalted be our Savior Lord –
   my Rock and One who saves.

[47] O God, it's You who will avenge,
   the One who will repay,
   Who brings the nations under me
   to follow and obey.

[48] You save me from my enemies,
   You lift me high above;
   You rescue me from those who hate
   because of Your great love.

[49] And so I'll always praise Your name
   to nations everywhere;
   A grateful song upon my lips
   I'll lift to You in prayer.

[50] For you uphold your king, O Lord,
   with victories in war;
   You show Your love for David's line
   both now and evermore.

Psalm 19

[1] The heavens show the work of God,
   His glory they proclaim;
   The skies disclose His handiwork
   through starry host aflame.

2 From day to day they make God known
    to those who dwell below;
While night to night revealing Him
    so all the world can know.

3 Although no speech or words are used
    to spread this through the land,
There is no nation, tribe, or soul
    that does not understand.

4 Their message goes to all the world,
    it's seen by everyone;
The heavens are God's handiwork,
    it's there He placed the sun.

5 The sun is like a happy groom
    who comes to greet the day,
Or like a youth who runs a race
    with joy the course to stay.

6 It rises with the morning dawn
    then sprints across the sky;
There's nothing that escapes its heat
    when shining from on high.

7 The Lord reveals His perfect law
    so every soul can grow;
His words are worthy of our trust,
    with wisdom all can know.

8 The statutes of the Lord are right,
    with joy for each new day;
And His commands are radiant –
    a light to show the way.

9 To fear the Lord is good and pure,
    enduring to the end;
The judgments of the Lord are sure
    and true as any friend.

¹⁰ They're lovelier than purest gold
 that anyone has known,
And sweeter still than honey sipped
 directly from the comb.

¹¹ They overflow with truth and grace
 and wisdom from the Lord;
So those who hear and follow them
 will reap a great reward.

¹² O Lord, we have so many faults
 and errors we don't see;
For every wrong where I am blind,
 forgive and set me free.

¹³ Deliver me from willful sins
 that keep me far from You;
Acquit me of transgressions, Lord,
 so I can start anew.

¹⁴ May every word that's in my mouth
 and thought within my soul,
Be pleasing in Your sight, O Lord,
 my Rock who makes me whole.

Psalm 20

¹ O may the Lord respond to you
 when troubles come your way;
May Jacob's God protect your life
 and keep you every day.

² May He supply abundant help
 when hearing your request;
May He send aid from Zion's hill
 so you are truly blessed.

³ May He recall your many gifts
 and holy sacrifice;
May He accept your offerings
 and find that they suffice.

⁴ May He provide your heart's request,
  the joy and hope you need;
 And may He guide you in your plans,
  ensuring they succeed.

⁵ When He delivers victory,
  our tongues will shout as one;
 We'll lift a banner in His name
  for what the Lord has done.

⁶ The Lord will surely help His king
  to rule throughout the land,
 From heaven giving victories
  by strength of His right hand.

⁷ Now some trust horse and chariot
  to help them through their plight;
 But we will put our trust in God
  and in His name delight.

⁸ For those who do not fear the Lord
  will fall and move no more;
 While those of us who love His name
  will rise and stand secure.

⁹ O Lord, we ask that You would give
  the king a victory;
 Please help us when we call to You
  in answer to our plea.

Psalm 21

¹ O Lord, the king is jubilant
  because You made him strong;
 He celebrates Your victories
  by bursting forth in song.

² You granted everything he asked –
  the cravings of his heart;
 Your grace will never leave him, Lord,
  Your joy will not depart.

³ You poured out blessings every day
    too lovely to behold;
And on his royal head You set
    a crown of purest gold.

⁴ The king requested only life,
    but more than this You gave;
You multiplied his days and years
    and kept him from the grave.

⁵ You granted mighty victories
    to make his glory great;
You gave him fame and majesty
    to be his true estate.

⁶ O surely You have blessed the king
    by Your eternal grace;
You filled him with Your presence, Lord,
    the joy of Your embrace.

⁷ Because he puts his trust in You –
    Your constant love and care;
He will not be unnerved by fear
    or fall into despair.

⁸ Your mighty hand and outstretched arm
    are raised against Your foes;
Your right hand finds and captures those
    who hate you and oppose.

⁹ Your anger burns like red-hot coals
    ignited by Your gaze,
Consuming every enemy
    within Your roaring blaze.

¹⁰ Descendants of Your foes will die,
    there's none who will survive;
You'll see that there are no more heirs,
    not one who's left alive.

¹¹ For though they schemed against You, Lord,
    to plot their wicked deed;
Their evil plan will not prevail,
    their hope will not succeed.

¹² Your hand will make them turn and run
    by drawing tight Your bow,
And scatter them both far and wide
    by striking with a blow.

¹³ We celebrate Your triumphs, Lord,
    and in Your strength rejoice;
We sing about Your mighty deeds
    and praise You with our voice.

Psalm 22

¹ My God, my God, why have You gone
    and left me all alone?
Why have You not delivered me
    or heard me when I groan?

² O Lord, my God, I cry to You
    at night and through the day;
I have no rest from calling You,
    for You seem far away.

³ And yet You are the Holy One,
    in majesty You dwell;
You are the hope of those You love,
    the praise of Israel.

⁴ Our ancestors entrusted You
    to keep them in Your care;
You reached Your hand and rescued them
    to free them from despair.

⁵ You heard their voices when they called
    and saved them when they cried;
Their trust in You was justified
    for You were on their side.

⁶ But I am like a lowly worm,
    not of the human race,
  Despised by everyone who sees
    and living in disgrace.

⁷ They shake their heads when seeing me,
    their scorn is unrestrained;
  They make disparaging remarks
    because I am disdained.

⁸ They say, *"You trusted in the Lord,*
    let's see if God saves you;
  If God delights in you so much,
    let's see Him bring you through."

⁹ But Lord, You saw me in the womb,
    You knew me from my birth;
  You made me put my trust in You
    from my first breath on earth.

¹⁰ Yes, from the day that I was born,
    my life was Yours alone;
  And You have always been my God,
    the only one I've known.

¹¹ So Lord, do not stay far away
    for danger is so near;
  There's no one else to comfort me,
    no one to calm my fear.

¹² My enemies are all around,
    in front and at my back;
  Like bulls of Bashan threatening,
    they circle in a pack.

¹³ They roar like lions on the hunt
    to demonstrate their might;
  They tear at me with open mouths
    to slay me with their bite.

¹⁴ Like water poured on sandy ground,
    my strength has disappeared;
My bones are sore and out of joint,
    my heart and mind are seared.

¹⁵ My arms are weaker than a pot
    of dried and brittle clay;
My tongue sticks tightly to my mouth;
    in dust like death I lay.

¹⁶ An evil mob is in pursuit
    like dogs that roam the lands;
They circle to devour me,
    they pierce my feet and hands.

¹⁷ My sunken flesh exposes bones
    till each of them I see;
My enemies look hard and stare
    while gloating over me.

¹⁸ They take the garments that I wear
    and gamble for each one;
They portion out the lot of them
    till I am left with none.

¹⁹ O Lord, do not be far away,
    do not be out of sight;
O You who are my only strength
    come quick to set things right.

²⁰ Deliver me from every sword,
    defend me from each knife;
Protect me from the teeth of dogs
    that seek to take my life.

²¹ O save me from the lion's grip
    with fangs that tear and bite;
And rescue me from horns of bulls
    that crush with all their might.

22 Then to the faithful I will shout
　　and glorify Your name;
　And when we meet to worship You,
　　I'll praise You once again.

23 So all of you who fear the Lord
　　come join with me in praise;
　Come Israel and Jacob too,
　　and those who know His ways.

24 For God has not despised the weak
　　nor scorned those in distress;
　He's never turned from those who call
　　to seek Him for redress.

25 When faithful people gather near,
　　I'll praise His name out loud;
　In front of those who fear the Lord,
　　I'll worship as I vowed.

26 The poor and destitute will eat
　　till they are satisfied;
　Then they will sing and praise the Lord
　　with hearts that are revived.

27 And people from throughout the earth
　　will turn back to the Lord;
　They'll glorify and worship Him,
　　and He will be adored.

28 For all the earth belongs to God –
　　the waters and the land;
　The nations too are under Him
　　and ruled by His command.

29 The wealthy and the prosperous
　　will feast and give Him praise;
　And those who mire in the dust
　　will thank the One who saves.

30 And generations yet to come
    will hear about His name;
And they will bow and serve the Lord
    so all will know His fame.

31 Their voices will be lifted up,
    informing everyone,
About the righteousness of God,
    and all the Lord has done.

Psalm 23

1 The Lord, my shepherd, cares for me
    and tends me like His sheep;
I do not want for anything,
    I'm safe within His keep.

2 He makes me lie and take my rest
    in green inviting fields;
He leads me near a quiet brook
    to which my spirit yields.

3 The Lord restores my life and soul
    and makes my pathways straight;
He leads me into righteousness
    because His name is great.

4 And though I walk through valleys deep
    with deathly shadows near,
Your rod and staff, they comfort me
    so I need never fear.

5 A table You prepare for me
    in front of all my foes;
My head with oil You anoint,
    my cup, it overflows.

6 O surely love and goodness, Lord,
    will always follow me;
And I will dwell within Your house
    for all eternity.

Psalm 24

¹ The Lord our God owns all the earth
   and everything within;
The animals and people too,
   they all belong to Him.

² He built it on the waters deep –
   the ocean far below;
He anchored it upon the seas
   where tides and currents flow.

³ So who can climb upon God's hill,
   approach His sacred space?
And who are they who hope to stand
   within His holy place?

⁴ The ones who come with spotless hands
   and hearts as pure as gold,
Who will not swear by what is false
   or to an idol hold.

⁵ Their eyes will see God's kindliness,
   the blessings of the Lord;
And He will call them innocent
   so they will be restored.

⁶ Such people are the ones who long
   to gaze upon His face;
They want to meet with Jacob's God,
   to know and taste His grace.

⁷ Lift up your heads, O mighty gates,
   O doors of ancient town,
To let the King of glory in
   and dwell when He comes down.

⁸ Who is this King so glorious
   who many long to see?
The Lord of strength, the Mighty One,
   who wins the victory.

⁹ Lift up your heads, O mighty gates,
  O doors of ancient town,
To let the King of glory in
  and dwell when He comes down.

¹⁰ Who is this King so glorious
  who many long to see?
The Lord who reigns and wears the crown,
  Almighty King is He.

Psalm 25

¹ To You, O Lord, I give my life
  because You make me whole;
To You alone I make this prayer
  by lifting up my soul.

² O God, I put my trust in You
  so keep me from the shame,
Of foes who triumph over me,
  then turn and mock my name.

³ No one will ever know disgrace
  who hopes in You alone;
But rebels will be beaten down
  for evil they have shown.

⁴ Reveal Your holy ways, O Lord,
  and make them known to me;
Illuminate the paths You set
  so they are clear to see.

⁵ Instruct me in the way of truth,
  then help me to obey;
For You're my Savior and the hope
  I trust in every day.

⁶ Remember, Lord, Your tenderness,
  the mercy that You show,
Your never changing love that comes
  from days of long ago.

7 Do not recall the times I've sinned,
    not living as I should;
But look on me with love and grace
    for You are always good.

8 O fair and gracious is the Lord,
    His righteousness is great;
He teaches sinners how to walk
    along a path that's straight.

9 He guides the humble in His way,
    He offers them His hand;
He leads them into what is true
    so they will understand.

10 The Lord reveals His faithful love
    to those who know His ways,
Who trust upon His covenant
    and keep it all their days.

11 O don't forsake Your promise, Lord,
    be faithful to Your name;
Forgive my sins, though they are great,
    and I am filled with shame.

12 If there are those who fear the Lord
    and what His hand can do,
Then He will teach them how to choose
    the path that's right and true.

13 And they will live their days in peace
    with riches of great worth;
And their descendants will be blessed,
    inheriting the earth.

14 The Lord is close to those who trust
    and hold His name in awe;
He tells them of His covenant
    and how to keep His law.

¹⁵ My eyes are always on the Lord
  to keep me from despair;
 He rescues me when I am trapped
  and lifts me from the snare.

¹⁶ So turn and show Your mercy, Lord,
  to one who is Your own;
 For I am weak and anguishing
  from suffering alone.

¹⁷ The sorrows of my heart have grown,
  my worries have increased;
 So help me till my pain is gone
  and troubles are released.

¹⁸ Consider my afflictions, Lord,
  my problems every day;
 Forgive me for the way I've erred,
  and take my sins away.

¹⁹ And look upon my enemies
  and how their numbers rise;
 O see how much they hate my life
  and seek my swift demise.

²⁰ Protect my soul and rescue me,
  deliver me from shame;
 For I find refuge in Your wings
  and trust upon Your name.

²¹ And when I put my confidence
  and hope in You, O Lord,
 Integrity will be my shield,
  and righteousness my sword.

²² So come, O God, to Israel,
  no longer stay Your hand;
 Deliver us from sorrows, Lord,
  and save this troubled land.

Psalm 26

[1] O Lord, please find me innocent
   because I do not stray;
I live a life of righteousness
   and trust in You each day.

[2] Please put me to the test, O Lord,
   and probe my heart and mind;
Look deeply and examine me,
   and judge the thoughts You find.

[3] Your love is ever close to me,
   Your kindness fills my heart;
I always walk within the truth
   that You alone impart.

[4] I pay no heed to hypocrites,
   their words I do not hear;
I turn away from those who lie
   whenever they appear.

[5] I loathe the wicked for their ways
   and evilness they spew;
I hate their immorality,
   the sinful things they do.

[6] I wash my hands in innocence
   to show that I am pure,
Then worship at Your altar, Lord,
   to let my spirit soar.

[7] And there I lift my voice to You
   with joyful shouts of praise;
I sing about Your awesome deeds
   and wonders of Your ways.

[8] O Lord, I love Your dwelling place,
   the house where You reside,
The shelter where Your glory dwells,
   the rest where You abide.

⁹ So do not let my soul despair
    or let my lifeblood spill;
But keep me far from those who hate
    and seek to maim and kill.

¹⁰ The wicked plot conspiracies
    and make their evil plans;
They force a bribe from all they meet,
    then clutch it in their hands.

¹¹ But as for me, I simply choose
    to do whatever's right;
O Lord, redeem me by Your grace
    and save me by Your might.

¹² My foot stands firm on solid ground
    because I've been restored;
And I will ever lift my voice
    to bless Your name, O Lord.

Psalm 27

¹ The Lord is my redeeming light,
    so who can frighten me?
The Lord protects me like a shield,
    from whom then shall I flee?

² For though the wicked seek my life
    like lions hunting prey,
They stumble when they come at me
    and quickly fall away.

³ And though my foes encircle me,
    my heart will never fear;
And even faced with coming war,
    I trust in God Who's near.

⁴ I ask the Lord for just one thing –
    to dwell within His place,
To seek Him in His temple courts
    and gaze upon His face.

⁵ For He will keep me safe from harm
    like one who guards a flock;
And in the shelter of His tent,
    He'll set me on a rock.

⁶ Then I will be victorious
    though foes encircle me;
And in His temple I will sing
    and praise him joyfully.

⁷ So hear me when I call, O Lord,
    please listen when I cry;
Be merciful by giving me
    Your answer in reply.

⁸ You beckon me to seek Your face
    and worship You anew;
And gladly does my heart respond
    by drawing near to You.

⁹ O Lord, don't let Your anger show,
    or hide from me, I pray;
O God my Savior, You're my help
    so do not turn away.

¹⁰ And though my parents turn from me
    and leave me in despair;
Still You, O Lord, are welcoming,
    and keep me in Your care.

¹¹ Direct me in the way to go –
    a path that's straight and clear;
And guide me from my enemies
    whenever they are near.

¹² O do not let my life be crushed
    and broken by my foes;
For they attack with lying tongues
    to magnify my woes.

¹³ O there is one thing that I know
and confident I'll see –
The awesome goodness of the Lord
poured out abundantly.

¹⁴ So trust the Lord and do not fear
the arrow or the sword;
But rather with a steadfast heart,
have faith, and trust the Lord.

Psalm 28

¹ O Lord, my Rock, I call to You,
do not ignore my plea;
For I will be like one who's died
if You don't answer me.

² O Lord, please hear my cry for help,
bestow Your grace anew,
As toward Your holy temple gates
I lift my hands to You.

³ Don't punish me with sinners, Lord,
whose evil does not cease,
Who mask the malice in their hearts
by speaking words of peace.

⁴ Rebuke the wicked for their deeds,
repay them everyone;
Exact a dear and costly price
for what their hands have done.

⁵ They do not care about the works
and wonders of the Lord;
So He will strike and crush them down
to never be restored.

⁶ O praise the Lord and worship Him
and lift His name on high;
For by His mercy and His grace,
He hears me when I cry.

⁷ The Lord protects me like a shield,
    I trust in Him each day;
And joyfully I sing His praise
    for showing me the way.

⁸ The Lord gives strength to those He loves,
    He guards them with His arm;
He fortifies His chosen king
    and keeps him safe from harm.

⁹ So save and bless Your people, Lord,
    embrace them from above;
And like a shepherd keep them safe,
    protected by Your love.

Psalm 29

¹ O praise the Lord, you mighty ones,
    with tributes and acclaim;
O honor Him for He is strong
    and worthy is His name.

² Yes, glorify and worship Him,
    His name forever bless;
In reverence bow down to Him
    in all His holiness.

³ The voice of God is in the deep
    and thunders a refrain;
It penetrates the darkest depths,
    then echoes back again.

⁴ The voice of God is powerful
    and issues His command;
The voice of God is glorious,
    magnificent and grand.

⁵ The voice of God reverberates,
    and mighty cedars fall;
It breaks the trees of Lebanon
    that once stood firm and tall.

⁶ The voice of God makes mountains skip
    like calves in early spring;
  Or like a goat that jumps about,
    attempting to take wing.

⁷ The voice of God strikes suddenly
    like lightning in the night;
  It flashes with unbounded force
    as darkness yields to light.

⁸ The voice of God shakes barren lands
    where earth is parched and dry,
  Like in the Kadesh desert plains
    where sands swirl to the sky.

⁹ The voice of God twists mighty oaks
    and strips the forests bare;
  So all within His temple sing
    His praise and glory there.

¹⁰ The Lord sits high above the deep
    where waves are tossed and thrown;
  Above the inundating floods,
    He rests upon His throne.

¹¹ The Lord attends to those He loves
    and makes their strength increase;
  He reassures and blesses them
    with joyfulness and peace.

Psalm 30

¹ O Lord, I praise You for Your grace
    that saved me from my foes,
  For keeping them from mocking me
    and gloating at my woes.

² O Lord my God, I called for You
    to help me in this land;
  You saw my tears and heard my cries,
    then healed me by Your hand.

³ O Lord, You kept me from the grave,
  a dark and fearful hole;
 You snatched me from the looming pit
  to save and keep my soul.

⁴ So let the saints sing to the Lord
  with voice and chorus raised;
 So that the holy name of God
  will be forever praised.

⁵ Although His anger comes and goes,
  His grace is never done;
 While weeping may consume the night,
  there's joy that greets the sun.

⁶ There was a time when I was safe,
  unshaken and secure;
 I felt that I could not be moved,
  and I would long endure.

⁷ For with Your blessing I was strong,
  a mountain without peer;
 But when You hid Your face from me,
  my heart was filled with fear.

⁸ O Lord, I called so You would hear
  and listen to my plea;
 I begged that mercy from Your hand
  would cover over me.

⁹ What good can come of my demise?
  What profit in my death?
 Will dust proclaim Your righteousness
  or praise You with its breath?

¹⁰ So hear, O Lord, with open ears
  my cry to You this day;
 O be my help and keeper, Lord,
  be merciful I pray.

11 For You have turned my brokenness
   to dancing in my soul;
Replacing tears and suffering
   with joy to make me whole.

12 So now my heart will sing to You,
   Your holy name I'll praise;
O Lord my God, I'll give You thanks
   both now and all my days.

Psalm 31

1 O Lord, in You I rest secure
   and safe in Your embrace;
Protect me through Your righteousness,
   and keep me from disgrace.

2 Please help me in my time of need,
   be quick to hear my call;
Deliver me and be my rock,
   a fortress strong and tall.

3 For You have been my refuge, Lord,
   a shelter every day;
So for the honor of Your name,
   direct me on my way.

4 Protect me from the trap that's set
   to catch me like a snare;
O be a hideaway from harm
   to keep me from despair.

5 I put my life into Your trust,
   my spirit in Your hands;
Redeem me by Your faithfulness
   and truth of Your commands.

6 My soul despises idols, Lord,
   and turns from those who do;
But I will hope upon Your name
   and always trust in You.

⁷ And in Your love, I'll dance for joy
   and sing a glad refrain,
Because You saw my broken soul
   and felt my anguished pain.

⁸ You have not let my enemies
   ensnare and capture me,
But set my feet on solid ground
   where I am safe and free.

⁹ So come now, Lord, be merciful,
   for I am filled with grief;
My eyes are red and drenched with tears,
   my body needs relief.

¹⁰ My days are spent in suffering,
   my life is on the wane;
My strength no longer carries me,
   my bones are filled with pain.

¹¹ My enemies have brought me down,
   my neighbors mock and jeer;
My friends are loath to look at me
   and flee when I am near.

¹² My name has been forgotten, Lord,
   as though I am no more;
I'm like an earthen water jar
   that's shattered on the floor.

¹³ I hear the sound of whispering
   by foes who stir up strife;
They execute their secret plans
   that seek to take my life.

¹⁴ Yet I have never strayed, O Lord,
   but put my trust in You,
Because You are the God I love,
   the One who sees me through.

¹⁵ My life is always in Your care,
    protected by Your hands;
So keep me safe from every foe
    who hunts me through the lands.

¹⁶ O cause Your face to shine on me
    with kindness from above;
Redeem me by Your tenderness
    and never-ending love.

¹⁷ Don't let me be disgraced, O Lord,
    for I have called Your name;
Dispatch the wicked to the grave,
    dishonored and in shame.

¹⁸ For they have spoken evil lies
    against what's true and pure;
So silence them for arrogance
    till they are heard no more.

¹⁹ How great the goodness You have planned
    and things that You have stored,
For those who trust and honor You
    and fear Your name, O Lord.

²⁰ Your arms will be a hideaway
    for those who are pursued,
A shelter from accusing tongues
    when evil words are spewed.

²¹ Receive the praises that I give
    and hear Your name be blessed,
Because You loved me when my soul
    was shattered and oppressed.

²² In my alarm, I thought You turned
    and walked away from me;
But You responded to my prayer
    and listened to my plea.

²³ So come now saints and love the Lord
    for watching over you,
And punishing the proud and smug
    for evil things they do.

²⁴ Forever keep your courage up,
    and always persevere;
For if you hope upon the Lord
    your heart will never fear.

Psalm 32

¹ How happy those whom God forgives
    and takes their sins away,
And those whom God exonerates
    when they have gone astray.

² How happy those who are absolved
    and pardoned by the Lord,
And in whose souls no lies are kept
    and no deceit is stored.

³ When I could not admit my sins,
    my bones grew weak and frail;
Throughout the day my spirit groaned,
    and hope began to fail.

⁴ O Lord, Your hand pressed down on me
    through endless nights and days;
My strength was sapped as if the sun
    had scorched me with its rays.

⁵ But when I told You of my sins
    and evil things I'd done,
You pardoned my transgressions, Lord,
    forgiving every one.

⁶ So may the godly pray to You
    when it begins to pour,
Protected from the rising flood
    and safe upon the shore.

⁷ O Lord, You are my hiding place
    when trouble comes along;
  You keep me far away from harm
    and fill me with a song.

⁸ The Lord will be a guide to those
    who follow in His way;
  He shows the path to walk along
    so none will go astray.

⁹ But don't be like a horse or mule
    that cannot understand,
  And needs a bit between its teeth
    to heed the least command.

¹⁰ For all the wicked suffer woes
    that drive them to despair;
  But those who trust upon the Lord
    receive His loving care.

¹¹ So come you righteous praise the Lord,
    with joy and gladness sing;
  And you with pure and upright hearts
    give glory to the King.

Psalm 33

¹ O sing unto the Lord, you saints,
    and make a joyful sound;
  And you, the righteous, praise His name,
    let every voice resound.

² Yes, make sweet music to the Lord,
    a melody that rings;
  O praise the Lord upon the lute
    and harp of many strings.

³ O sing a new song to the Lord
    with joy that greets His ear;
  And play it with a skillful hand
    so every note is clear.

4 The Lord has shown His word is right,
   forever good and true;
 In everything that He has done,
   His faithfulness shines through.

5 The Lord loves truth and righteousness,
   and justice He'll defend;
 The earth shows forth His steadfast love,
   abundant to the end.

6 The Lord created, by His word,
   the heavens and the sky;
 He breathed and all the stars were formed
   that shine down from on high.

7 The Lord collected in one place
   the waters of the sea;
 And like a storehouse in the deep,
   preserves them carefully.

8 The Lord is great and wonderful
   and worthy of acclaim;
 Let everyone who has a breath
   give honor to His name.

9 The Lord God spoke, and all the earth
   appeared the way He planned –
 The mountains, plains and waters deep
   by word of His command.

10 The Lord stops nations and their schemes,
   He brings them to an end;
 He thwarts the goals and purposes
   on which their hopes depend.

11 But all the plans the Lord has made
   forever will endure;
 The purposes that come from Him
   are definite and sure.

¹² How happy will a nation be
      that trusts upon the Lord;
   How joyful will its people be
      when they have been restored.

¹³ The Lord in heaven far above
      looks out and gazes down,
   To see those living on the earth,
      in countryside and town.

¹⁴ And from His dwelling place on high,
      He watches those below,
   Observing everyone of us
      wherever we may go.

¹⁵ The Lord has fashioned every heart,
      He knows the thoughts of all;
   He thinks about the things we do,
      no matter great or small.

¹⁶ An army cannot save a king
      or keep his foes at bay;
   No warrior by strength alone
      can ever get away.

¹⁷ And neither can the bravest horse
      that's battle strong and fit,
   Deliver anyone who hopes
      or puts their trust in it.

¹⁸ The Lord forever keeps His eyes
      on those who fear His name;
   He watches those who seek His love
      and on it make their claim.

¹⁹ For God delivers us from death,
      from misery and pain;
   He keeps us fed in times of want
      when there has been no rain.

²⁰ And so in faith we wait and hope
    by trusting in the Lord;
For He's our help in time of need,
    a shield from every sword.

²¹ Our heart and soul delight in Him,
    rejoicing in His peace;
When trusting in His holy name,
    our spirit finds release.

²² O Lord, please let Your love descend
    and on us gently rest;
So as we place our hope in You
    our lives are richly blessed.

Psalm 34

¹ I will forever thank the Lord
    and bless His holy name;
His praises will be on my lips,
    His glory I'll proclaim.

² My soul will boast upon the Lord
    and tell about His might;
So those afflicted and oppressed
    will hear and take delight.

³ O join with me and praise the Lord
    so He is glorified;
Together let us lift His name
    with praises far and wide.

⁴ When I was down and sought the Lord,
    He heard me through my tears,
Then by His hand delivered me
    from all my deepest fears.

⁵ For those who look upon the Lord
    will feel His warm embrace;
Their faces will be radiant
    and never know disgrace.

⁶ When suffering, I begged the Lord
    to listen to my plea;
  Then from my trouble and distress,
    His hand delivered me.

⁷ The angels of the Lord abide
    with those who fear His name;
  And He will surely rescue them
    and keep their lives from shame.

⁸ So taste and see the Lord is good,
    and hope in Him alone;
  For happy those who trust His grace
    and mercies He has shown.

⁹ And you, His saints, exalt the Lord
    and live in awe of Him;
  For those who honor and obey
    have joy that will not dim.

¹⁰ A lion may grow weak and faint
    when hungry for a kill;
  But those who seek to know the Lord
    will always have their fill.

¹¹ So come now children, hear my voice
    so I am not ignored;
  I'll teach you how to worship God,
    the way to fear the Lord.

¹² For if you want to have a life
    with long and joyful days,
  Then here are things that you should do
    as guidance for your ways.

¹³ Refrain from speaking evil words
    that tear the soul apart;
  Don't tell a lie or ever keep
    deception in your heart.

¹⁴ Reject and turn from wickedness,
    pursue what's good and pure;
Seek peace and justice every day
    till conflict is no more.

¹⁵ The Lord is looking at the just
    and righteous in the lands;
He pays attention to their cries
    because He understands.

¹⁶ His hand has turned against the vile
    to censure and condemn;
So when they die, no one recalls
    or thinks again of them.

¹⁷ The righteous call upon the Lord
    Who hears their raised alarm;
He sooths their troubles and their fears,
    protecting them from harm.

¹⁸ He knows each brokenhearted soul,
    He's close to the distressed;
He makes the wounded spirit whole
    and gives the weary rest.

¹⁹ Although the good and virtuous
    may fall and suffer much,
The Lord delivers all of them
    and heals them with His touch.

²⁰ The Lord preserves the pure in heart
    whenever they're attacked;
He keeps their bodies safe from harm
    so not a bone is cracked.

²¹ The wicked though will be destroyed,
    by evil they'll be slain;
The enemies of righteousness
    will suffer guilt and pain.

22 But servants of the Lord will know
  redemption in their soul;
 For those who trust in Him are saved
  and once again made whole.

Psalm 35

1 Oppose those who oppose me, Lord,
  and with my foes contend;
 O fight those who are fighting me
  to make this conflict end.

2 Arise, O Lord, deliver me,
  and hurry to my aid;
 Take up a shield in my defense
  to block the sharpest blade.

3 O draw Your sword and javelin
  as foes attack this place;
 Assure my soul by promising,
  "I am your saving grace."

4 May those who try to take my life
  be shamed for their deceit;
 May those who plot their evil schemes
  be turned back in defeat.

5 May they be tossed and blown like chaff
  upon a windy day;
 And may Your angel scatter them
  to regions far away.

6 May they be lost upon a path
  that's slippery and black,
 Your angel ever threatening
  while close upon their track.

7 Though unprovoked, they set a trap
  to catch me unaware;
 They dug a pit along my path
  to snag me like a snare.

⁸ O may their own nets tangle them
    and grab them by surprise;
May they fall deep into the pit
    to meet their sure demise.

⁹ For surely then my soul will sing
    and in the Lord delight;
For He has won the victory
    and saved me by His might.

¹⁰ And from the depths my soul will ask,
    "Is any like You, Lord?
You help the poor and save the weak
    from those who wield the sword."

¹¹ Yet evil witnesses appear
    with words that are not true,
Accusing me of heinous crimes
    and things I did not do.

¹² For they repay with evil deeds,
    my kindly acts and care;
Which leaves my soul distraught and drained,
    in anguish and despair.

¹³ Yet in the past when they were ill,
    I fasted faithfully;
I bowed my head and prayed for them
    in all humility.

¹⁴ I grieved for them as if they were
    a brother or a friend;
I wept as though my mother's life
    had met a sudden end.

¹⁵ But when I stumbled, they approached
    and gathered round with glee,
Their lips forever slandering,
    their tongues berating me.

¹⁶ Like those who do not fear the Lord,
    they treated me with scorn;
  Their gnashing teeth were full of hate,
    which left my soul forlorn.

¹⁷ How long, O Lord, before You come?
    How long will You delay?
  O rescue me from those who strike
    like lions crush their prey.

¹⁸ O how I want to praise Your name
    in front of all the saints,
  And gather with Your people, Lord,
    to give You all my thanks.

¹⁹ So do not let my enemies
    rejoice at my demise;
  And do not let them shout for joy
    at sorrow in my eyes.

²⁰ They are not gracious with their tongues,
    deceit is all they speak;
  They slander those who live in peace –
    the gentle and the meek.

²¹ With open mouths they stare at me,
    with evil tongues pursue;
  Excitedly they jeer and taunt,
    "See what's become of you!"

²² Arise, O Lord, for You have seen
    how I've become their prey;
  Speak out and end Your reticence,
    do not be far away.

²³ Arouse Yourself to my defense,
    awaken to my plight;
  Take up my cause, my Lord and God,
    and help me by Your might.

^{24} Because You are a righteous judge,
　　adjudicate my case;
Don't let my enemies rejoice
　　and see me in disgrace.

^{25} Don't let them think about themselves,
　　"O we will have our way."
Don't let them chant with gloating tongues,
　　"Our plans have won the day."

^{26} May all who smile at my distress
　　be stigmatized and shamed;
May those who feel superior
　　be slandered and defamed.

^{27} But may those cheering when I'm cleared,
　　shout loudly, *"Praise the Lord!*
For He has made His servant whole,
　　with life and health restored."

^{28} O Lord, You are the righteous God
　　I'll worship all my days;
Forever I will honor You
　　and lift Your name in praise.

Psalm 36

^{1} The wicked are awash in sin,
　　which fills their heart and mind;
They do not know the fear of God,
　　to Him their eyes are blind.

^{2} They fool themselves with flattery
　　and don't regret their sin;
Their eyes refuse to look upon
　　the evil that's within.

^{3} They never speak a truthful word,
　　their mouths are full of lies;
All goodness has deserted them,
　　their judgments are unwise.

4 For even when the morning dawns
    they plan their evil way,
Which sets them on a wrongful path
    of sin throughout their day.

5 But, Lord, Your love is limitless,
    it reaches to the sky;
Your faithfulness is taller still
    than clouds that float on high.

6 Your righteousness is towering
    like mountains looming tall;
Your justice like the deepest seas
    gives life and hope to all.

7 Your endless love is priceless, Lord,
    the treasure trove of kings;
Your people hide within Your keep
    and shadow of Your wings.

8 They feast upon the food You bring
    and savor every bite;
They quench their thirst from flowing streams
    and rivers of delight.

9 For Lord, You are the fount and well
    of life as it should be;
You shine more brightly than the sun,
    revealing all we see.

10 So always show Your love to those
    who tightly cling to You;
Extend Your righteousness to all
    whose hearts are ever true.

11 Do not allow the proud to strike
    or crush me by their might;
And do not let them raise their hand
    so I am put to flight.

[12] But see the way the wicked fall
    and meet their just demise;
They lie where they are beaten down,
    unable to arise.

Psalm 37

[1] Do not allow yourself to fret
    when evil seems to win,
Nor envy anyone who gains
    from wickedness and sin.

[2] For they will wither like the grass
    on dry and windswept plains,
And fade away like tender plants
    without the springtime rains.

[3] O trust the Lord in everything,
    and always do what's right;
Live safely in the land He gave,
    and in it take delight.

[4] Find pleasure and contentedness
    by drawing near the Lord;
Then what your heart desires most
    will be your just reward.

[5] Commit your way and life to God,
    stay on the narrow path;
And trust the Lord in everything
    to act on your behalf.

[6] Then He will make your righteousness
    be like the dawn's first ray,
Your virtue shining over all
    like sun that lights the day.

[7] Be still and wait upon the Lord,
    let not your spirit fail;
And do not fret when wicked schemes
    and evil plots prevail.

⁸ Don't fill your heart with wrath and spite,
   or let it take alarm;
For anger leads to evilness,
   anxiety to harm.

⁹ But those who wait upon the Lord
   will surely own the land;
While those who act maliciously
   are cut off by His hand.

¹⁰ The wicked soon will pass away,
   their reign of evil done;
And though you search and look for them,
   you won't discover one.

¹¹ The humble and the meek will live
   and flourish in the land –
A place where they can feel secure
   and peace is close at hand.

¹² The wicked plot against the just
   and plan their evil ways;
They bare their teeth and spew forth rage
   that scorches like a blaze.

¹³ The Lord God laughs at all they do,
   to Him one thing is clear –
Their end is coming very soon,
   the time is drawing near.

¹⁴ The wicked draw their sharpened swords
   and deftly string their bows,
To kill the righteous and the poor,
   and all whom they oppose.

¹⁵ But their own sword will turn on them
   and penetrate their heart;
Their bows and armaments will fail
   as they are ripped apart.

¹⁶ Much better to be destitute
    and always do what's right,
Than prosper with abundant wealth
    achieved by fraud and spite.

¹⁷ The Lord provides the just with strength
    to help them through the day,
But breaks the wicked of their grip
    until they fall away.

¹⁸ The Lord observes the virtuous,
    the righteous and the pure;
Their legacy will never fade
    and ever will endure.

¹⁹ When times are bad they will not fall
    or wither like a reed;
When famine strikes and food is scarce,
    they'll never be in need.

²⁰ The Lord will strike the wicked down
    and slay them with a stroke;
Like fields of dry and burning grass,
    they'll vanish into smoke.

²¹ The wicked borrow by deceit,
    not planning to repay;
The righteous share from grateful hearts
    by giving much away.

²² The Lord will bless the good and just,
    bequeathing them the land;
The Lord will curse the bad and vile
    and smite them by His hand.

²³ The Lord takes joy in those He loves,
    their way is His delight;
He steadies and supports the plans
    of those whose steps are right.

²⁴ And though they stumble on their path,
    they will not hit the ground;
The Lord will hold them with His hand
    to keep their bodies sound.

²⁵ Though I was young and now am old,
    I know the Lord is true;
He keeps the righteous near to Him
    and feeds their children too.

²⁶ The just are always generous,
    with kindness as their way;
Their children are a gift to them,
    a blessing every day.

²⁷ So turn from wrong and evil deeds,
    and always do what's right;
And you will live within the land,
    forever in God's sight.

²⁸ For God loves those who seek the truth,
    who trust and never doubt;
But offspring of the vile He spurns,
    He strikes and drives them out.

²⁹ The righteous will receive the land,
    a promise from the Lord –
A good and just inheritance
    to live in evermore.

³⁰ The righteous speak with words of truth,
    from tongues forever wise;
They talk with justice in their souls,
    discernment in their eyes.

³¹ The righteous have the law of God
    engraven on their heart;
They do not trip or lose their way
    or from His path depart.

³² The wicked spy upon the good
    and righteous on their way;
They lie in wait and bide their time
    till they can strike and slay.

³³ But God does not forsake His saints
    or leave them to the vile;
Nor will He let them be condemned
    if they are brought to trial.

³⁴ So trust the Lord and keep His way,
    and you will own the land;
Your eyes will see the wicked struck
    and cut off by His hand.

³⁵ For I once saw the wicked thrive
    and flourish like a tree;
They towered over everyone
    as far as I could see.

³⁶ But later on I passed their way,
    and though I looked around,
They disappeared without a trace,
    not ever to be found.

³⁷ So think about the good and pure
    and those who do what's right;
Their future is a place of hope,
    that's filled with peace and light.

³⁸ Then think about the bad and vile,
    the wicked and their hate;
Their future is abandonment,
    destruction is their fate.

³⁹ The righteous have a saving grace
    that's from the Lord alone;
For He's the strength in troubled times
    for those who are His own.

^{40} The Lord is close to those He loves,
    He hears them when they cry;
He saves them from all evilness
    whenever they draw nigh.

Psalm 38

^{1} O Lord, do not admonish me
    or let Your anger show;
Do not rebuke me in Your wrath
    or strike me with a blow.

^{2} For You have let Your arrows fly
    and guided them in flight;
You've pierced me with their sharpened tips
    and crushed me by Your might.

^{3} My flesh grows weak from Your reproach,
    I suffer many pains;
My bones are frail from how I've sinned,
    no health in them remains.

^{4} My sin has overwhelmed my soul
    like one who's bound and chained;
My guilt is much too hard to bear
    and cannot be restrained.

^{5} My wounds are raw and festering
    like lesions on the skin;
They're horrid and detestable
    because of all my sin.

^{6} My frame is bent and twisted low,
    no longer am I strong;
In misery I go about
    in mourning all day long.

^{7} My sides are gripped with searing pain,
    I yearn for some relief;
My body is approaching death,
    my soul is filled with grief.

⁸ My suffering has weakened me
  and stripped away all hope;
 My heart cries out with mournful groans,
  no longer can I cope.

⁹ My yearnings and my deepest wants
  are known to You, O Lord;
 Don't let the sighing of my heart
  be hidden or ignored.

¹⁰ My heart is pounding in my chest,
  my strength is all but gone;
 My eyes have lost their brightness, Lord,
  their light has been withdrawn.

¹¹ My friends and neighbors hide from me
  because of all my sores;
 My family stays far away
  like veiled and distant shores.

¹² My enemies lay traps and snares
  to crush and ruin me;
 They make their plans and spread their lies
  and plot their treachery.

¹³ My tongue cannot communicate,
  it cannot speak a sound;
 My mind is numb to every thought
  and deaf to all around.

¹⁴ My senses have deserted me,
  my ears no longer hear;
 No words can form upon my lips,
  no sounds from them appear.

¹⁵ But yet I wait on You, O Lord,
  and hope in You alone;
 I know that You will answer me
  because I am Your own.

¹⁶ I've said to You, *"Don't let my foes*
    take joy at my demise,
or laugh when seeing how I've slipped,
    unable to arise."

¹⁷ For I am close to falling down,
    about to pass away;
My sorrows never leave my side,
    I suffer every day.

¹⁸ I'm conscious of my many sins,
    and these I have confessed;
But still I'm troubled by my wrongs,
    I'm anguished and distressed.

¹⁹ My enemies are strong and fierce
    and ready for a fight,
But they've no cause for hating me
    or reason for their spite.

²⁰ They slander and disparage me,
    opposing all that's true,
Returning evil for the good
    and righteous things I do.

²¹ O Lord, do not abandon me,
    "Forsake me not," I cry;
Do not be far away from me,
    but come and venture nigh.

²² O Lord, my Savior, hurry here
    and do not be delayed;
Come quickly now and rescue me,
    O hasten to my aid.

Psalm 39

¹ I pledged to watch the way I act
    and never speak a lie,
To place a guard upon my lips
    when those who sin pass by.

² And so I kept a silent watch
    where all my talking ceased;
But yet my suffering grew worse
    and misery increased.

³ My heart was smoldering within,
    I felt like I would choke;
The more I thought, the more I burned,
    until at last I spoke.

⁴ O tell me, Lord, when will I die?
    How many are my years?
How many days do I have left
    until my end appears?

⁵ For You have made my time too short,
    my years rush swiftly by;
Each person's life is but a breath
    that passes with a sigh.

⁶ For we are shadows in the night,
    we work ourselves in vain;
We strive for wealth and pile it up
    for other people's gain.

⁷ O Lord, for what then do I wait?
    How is it I can cope?
It's You where I have placed my trust
    for You alone give hope.

⁸ So rescue me from all my sins,
    deliver me I pray;
Don't let the foolish show contempt
    or have the final say.

⁹ For I do not respond to them
    because, O Lord, I know,
That You alone have done these things
    that make me suffer so.

10 O Lord, remove Your scourge from me,
   and pain I can't withstand;
For I am perishing from blows
   delivered by Your hand.

11 For Your rebuke is like a moth
   that eats a closet bare,
Reducing us to what we are –
   mere vapor in the air.

12 So hear, O Lord, my cries for help,
   O let them reach Your ear;
For I am like my ancestors
   and only briefly here.

13 Please turn away Your discipline,
   show mercy I implore;
That I may know a little joy
   before I am no more.

Psalm 40

1 I waited calmly for the Lord
   to listen to my plea,
Until at last He turned His head
   and bent His ear toward me.

2 He pulled me from the miry clay,
   a pit of sinking sand;
He set my feet upon a rock,
   a solid place to stand.

3 He put a new song in my mouth,
   a song to sing His praise;
So all will see and fear His name
   and trust Him all their days.

4 For they are blessed who trust the Lord
   and to His name are true,
Who do not worship foreign gods
   or join with those who do.

⁵ O Lord, the wonders You have done
   are marvelous and fair;
Too many are Your deeds to count,
   too many to declare.

⁶ No sacrifice or offering
   did You demand or seek;
But You have opened up my ears
   so I could hear You speak.

⁷ And when I heard Your voice, I said,
   "I'm here Lord, as You see;
I've come to do what's in the law
   and what You ask of me.

⁸ *For I delight to do Your will,*
   and from it won't depart,
Because Your law is in my mind
   and written on my heart."

⁹ O I proclaim Your righteousness
   to those who are Your own;
I never stop from sharing it
   to make Your goodness known.

¹⁰ I do not make a secret, Lord,
   of Your astounding love;
But I declare Your faithfulness
   and rescue from above.

¹¹ So do not spare Your charity,
   and do not hide Your grace;
But hold me by Your love and truth,
   secure in Your embrace.

¹² For countless troubles hem me in,
   my life is torn apart;
More than the hairs upon my head
   are sins within my heart.

¹³ O come now, Lord, and rescue me,
    deliver me I cry;
Be merciful and save my life,
    come quickly and draw nigh.

¹⁴ May those who seek to take my life
    be thoroughly ashamed;
And those delighting in my pain
    be turned back and defamed.

¹⁵ And may those making sport of me
    and treating me with scorn,
Be shamed and humbled in defeat,
    embarrassed and forlorn.

¹⁶ But may those seeking after You,
    who in Your love rejoice,
Forever say *"The Lord is great,"*
    together with one voice.

¹⁷ O I am weak and needy, Lord,
    so think of me today;
For surely You're my only hope,
    so hurry, don't delay.

Psalm 41

¹ O happy those whose hearts are moved
    to help the poor and weak;
The Lord will rescue them from harm
    when times are looking bleak.

² The Lord protects and blesses them
    because their lives are dear;
He will not leave them on their own
    when enemies appear.

³ The Lord sustains and watches them
    whenever fever burns;
He tends them in their maladies
    till health and strength returns.

⁴ I said, *"I've sinned against You, Lord,*
and wandered from Your way;
So let Your mercy overflow
to heal my soul today."

⁵ My enemies are cruel to me,
I'm hated and harassed.
They ask, *"When will he meet his end?*
When will he breathe his last?"

⁶ And those who come to visit me
speak only with deceit;
They probe for news of my decline
as slander to repeat.

⁷ My enemies are secretive,
they hope for my demise;
They don't desire good for me
but whisper wicked lies.

⁸ They say I have a dread disease,
that in death's grip I dwell;
They say I'll not rise up again,
that I will not get well.

⁹ And even my devoted friend,
the one I thought was true,
The one who shared my food and drink
has turned against me too.

¹⁰ O pour Your grace upon me, Lord,
and do not turn away;
Be merciful and give me strength
to beat my foes today.

¹¹ I know that You are watchful, Lord,
and satisfied with me;
For never has my enemy
obtained the victory.

¹² And since my heart is innocent,
　　Your mercy lifts my soul;
　　You keep me in Your presence, Lord,
　　so I am ever whole.

¹³ So praise the God of Israel,
　　the Lord who has no end;
　　From evermore to evermore
　　shout Amen and Amen.

Psalm 42

¹ Just as the deer is panting hard
　　for water flowing streams,
　　My soul pants hard for You, O God,
　　for You alone it dreams.

² My soul thirsts for the living God,
　　it's desperate for the Lord;
　　When will I ever see His face –
　　the One whom I've adored?

³ My tears have been my only food
　　at night and through the day,
　　While people say, *"Where is your God?*
　　Why does He stay away?"

⁴ My heart is broken as I think
　　of other festive days,
　　Of entering the house of God
　　with joyful shouts of praise.

⁵ Yet why, my soul, are you distressed?
　　And why do you despair?
　　In God my Savior I will hope
　　and praise Him for His care.

⁶ For when my soul is feeling down
　　and when its strength is through,
　　From Jordan's flats to Hermon's heights
　　I'll think of God anew.

7 I'll hear a sound like roaring seas
    where deep calls out to deep;
I'll feel His waves and breakers crash
    as over me they sweep.

8 The Lord pours out His love by day
    and gives a song at night,
A song so sweet, that it's my prayer
    to God, my guiding light.

9 But now I cry to God my Rock,
    "Have You forgotten me?
Must I forever mourn the hurts
    caused by the enemy?"

10 The insults of my foes cut deep
    like bones pierced by a spear;
Their words continue day and night,
    "Where is your God?" they sneer.

11 Yet why, my soul, are you distressed?
    And why do you despair?
In God my Savior I will hope
    and praise Him for His care.

Psalm 43

1 O God, defend and judge my cause
    against those hating You;
Protect me from their wickedness
    and evil things they do.

2 O why have You rejected me
    when once You were my keep?
And why must foes oppress me till
    I'm broken down and weep?

3 Just send Your truth to shine on me,
    O let it be my guide,
To bring me to Your holy hill,
    the place where You abide.

4 Then to Your altar I will go
　　for joyful are Your ways;
　I'll play the harp, O God, my God,
　　with songs that give You praise.

5 So why, my soul, are you distressed?
　　Why are you in despair?
　In God my Savior I will hope
　　and praise Him for His care.

Psalm 44

1 O God, You once displayed Your might
　　in days of long ago;
　Our ancestors revealed these things
　　ensuring we would know.

2 You crushed the heathen nations, Lord,
　　and drove them from the land;
　You made Your people prosper there
　　by power of Your hand.

3 They did not win the land by skill,
　　by sword, or by their might,
　But by the strength of Your right hand,
　　Your mercy, and Your light.

4 O Lord, You are our God and King,
　　the One whom we profess,
　The One who guided Jacob's path,
　　securing his success.

5 Through You we crush our enemies,
　　with You we bring them low;
　And by the power of Your name,
　　we trample every foe.

6 We do not trust in blade or bow
　　or hope in sword or shield;
　For these will not a triumph bring
　　nor make our rivals yield.

⁷ It's You Who gives us victory,
    which gladly we proclaim;
You rescue us when danger lurks
    and put our foes to shame.

⁸ To You, O God, we make this pledge –
    to thank You all our days;
We glorify and honor You
    and lift Your name in praise.

⁹ Yet now You have rejected us
    and left us to our plight;
You do not help our armies, Lord,
    when marching out to fight.

¹⁰ You drove us from the battlefield
    to places far away;
Our adversaries plundered us
    like lions eat their prey.

¹¹ You let us be devoured, Lord,
    like unattended sheep;
You scattered us throughout the lands,
    no longer in Your keep.

¹² You sold us for a widow's mite,
    a short weight on a scale;
You priced us far below our worth
    with no gain on the sale.

¹³ You let our neighbors scoff at us,
    to look our way and sneer;
We hear the taunts and mocking scorn
    from those who gather near.

¹⁴ You made our name be ridiculed
    so people shake their heads,
A joke to nations everywhere
    as our dishonor spreads.

¹⁵ We find ourselves discredited
　　and living in disgrace;
　　While all day long we hang our heads
　　with shame upon our face.

¹⁶ For being taunted and reviled
　　is currently our fate;
　　Our enemies are bent on spite,
　　vindictiveness and hate.

¹⁷ But why O God did this occur?
　　We'd not forgotten You.
　　We always kept Your covenant,
　　remaining ever true.

¹⁸ For never had our hearts turned back,
　　nor had our footsteps strayed;
　　No, never had we wandered, Lord,
　　from off the path You made.

¹⁹ But You abandoned us to lands
　　where prowling jackals bark,
　　A place where deathly shadows roam
　　in bleakness and the dark.

²⁰ O God, if we had turned from You
　　and never sung Your praise,
　　Or raised our hands to foreign gods
　　to follow in their ways –

²¹ Then surely You'd discover this,
　　it could not be denied;
　　You know the secrets of our hearts,
　　there's nothing we can hide.

²² Yet for Your sake we stare at death,
　　we suffer and we weep;
　　We're led away to slaughter, Lord,
　　condemned to die like sheep.

²³ Awake, O Lord, and sleep no more,
   be shaken and arise;
Do not reject us anymore,
   but listen to our cries;

²⁴ No longer hide Your face from us,
   no longer close Your ears;
Do not forget our misery,
   adversity and fears.

²⁵ For deeply are we in distress,
   to dust our souls are bound;
Our bodies have been trampled on
   and lay upon the ground.

²⁶ So rise up, Lord, and rescue us,
   come quickly to this place;
Redeem us by Your endless love
   and Your unfailing grace.

Psalm 45

¹ There is a song that fills my soul
   with joy that overflows;
The king will hear me sing aloud
   these verses I compose.

² O king, you are the fairest one
   of all the sons of men;
Your lips are blessed by God with grace
   so they can shout amen.

³ You strap a sword upon your side,
   O brave and mighty king;
You clothe yourself majestically,
   an eagle taking wing.

⁴ You ride defending righteousness,
   arrayed in dignity;
You lift your hand for what is just
   and gain the victory.

⁵ Your sharpened arrows pierce the hearts
   of those who are your foes;
 The nations fall beneath your feet,
   defeated by Your blows.

⁶ You govern from the ageless throne
   established by God's hand;
 The scepter of your kingdom's rule
   is justice in the land.

⁷ You take delight in righteousness,
   but vileness you deplore;
 So God has set you over kings
   to make your spirit soar.

⁸ You put on robes infused with myrrh
   and spices that beguile;
 In palaces of ivory,
   sweet music makes you smile.

⁹ The daughters of nobility
   are honored in your fold;
 Your royal bride is at your side,
   bedecked in finest gold.

¹⁰ O daughter, you will be his bride
   so hear what I espouse;
 Forget your family and your ways,
   forget your parents' house.

¹¹ The king will see your loveliness,
   and you will be adored;
 So honor and obey the king
   for he is now your lord.

¹² Your favor will be sought by all,
   by people of great means;
 From Tyre they'll bring many gifts
   befitting lofty queens.

¹³ How glorious the princess bride
    who's ready to be wed;
Her gown is of the choicest cloth,
    and laced with golden thread.

¹⁴ Adorned in her embroidered robe,
    she comes to meet the king;
And many maids attend to her
    while in their hearts they sing.

¹⁵ With joy and gladness she is led
    as they proceed along;
They enter through the palace gates,
    a happy joyous throng.

¹⁶ O king, your sons will take your place
    by word of your command;
And you will make each one a prince
    to rule throughout the land.

¹⁷ Your story will be told in ways
    that no one can ignore;
So every nation will recall,
    and praise you evermore.

Psalm 46

¹ Our God's a refuge and our strength
    and always at our side,
A timely help when trouble comes,
    an ever-present guide.

² Although the earth erupts in quakes,
    we will not shake or fear;
Though glaciers crash into the sea,
    our God is always near.

³ And though the oceans roar and foam,
    and breakers crash and swell,
Though mountains sway and split in two,
    we know that all is well.

⁴ There is a river known as joy
   that flows through streets of gold;
 It brings the city of our God
   delight and bliss untold.

⁵ And in His city God resides
   so ever it will stand;
 For He is there when morning dawns
   to hold it in His hand.

⁶ The nations drop and kingdoms fall
   with shouting and a crash;
 God lifts His voice unto the earth
   and melts it in a flash.

⁷ The God of Jacob is our shield,
   a fortress strong as stone;
 The Lord our God is by our side
   so we are not alone.

⁸ Come see the things the Lord has done,
   and judge them by their worth,
 The desolations He has brought
   for justice on the earth.

⁹ The Lord breaks bows and shatters shields
   and brings an end to war;
 He smashes every armament
   till conflict is no more.

¹⁰ He says, *"I will be known by all
   and lifted high on wings;
 Be still and know that I am God
   who reigns above all kings."*

¹¹ The God of Jacob is our shield,
   a fortress strong as stone;
 The Lord our God is by our side
   so we are not alone.

Psalm 47

1 O come now people clap your hands
    and join the festive throngs;
  Come shout to God and sing His praise
    with loud and joyful songs.

2 The Lord Most High is wonderful,
    there's none of greater worth,
  The highest and the grandest King,
    He reigns above the earth.

3 The Lord gives us the victory
    by power of His hand;
  He brings the nations under us
    by word of His command.

4 He chooses our inheritance
    to make His kindness known,
  A land that we, as Jacob's seed,
    can settle as our own.

5 The Lord ascends to mountain heights
    while people cheer His name,
  With trumpet blasts and joyful shouts,
    approval and acclaim.

6 O sing to God who reigns on high,
    sing songs with voices raised;
  Yes, sing to Him, our noble King,
    and let His name be praised.

7 For God is King of all the earth
    so sing Him songs that please;
  Sing psalms and hymns and spirituals
    with sweetest melodies.

8 God rules the nations near and far,
    He governs them alone;
  He issues His decrees and laws
    from on His holy throne.

⁹ The nations join with God's elect,
 together drawing nigh;
They come because He reigns supreme
 and judges from on high.

Psalm 48

¹ The Lord is great and over all,
 and worthy to be praised;
Within the city of our God,
 sweet songs to Him are raised.

² O high above where all is fair
 and eagles take to wing,
Mount Zion looms majestically,
 the city of the King.

³ And there inside its palace gates,
 resplendent and immense,
He shows Himself to be its shield,
 its stronghold and defense.

⁴ Now many were the foreign kings
 advancing to attack,
Who joined their forces for the fight
 like jackals in a pack.

⁵ But when they saw God's citadel,
 it filled them with dismay,
So massive and formidable,
 they turned to run away.

⁶ But they were seized with trembling,
 their hearts were gripped by fear,
Like suffering from labor pains
 when birth is drawing near.

⁷ God overwhelmed and shattered them
 so they could not prevail,
Like ships torn by a storm at sea,
 a fleet caught in a gale.

⁸ For in His city we observed
    what we'd heard all along –
That God protects it by His hand,
    a hand that's sure and strong.

⁹ And in God's holy temple court,
    a place set high above,
We come to pray and meditate
    on His unfailing love.

¹⁰ We lift the name of God our Lord
    and gladly sing His praise;
The righteousness of His right hand
    reveals His awesome ways.

¹¹ And from Mount Zion's lofty perch
    to Judah's dusty towns,
His righteous judgments are proclaimed
    with many joyful sounds.

¹² So count its towers when you walk
    through Zion's hills and streets;
Consider its magnificence,
    and contemplate its feats.

¹³ And think about its parapets,
    observe its citadel,
So future generations know
    and love Mount Zion well.

¹⁴ For God has shown that He's our God,
    an ever-present friend;
Forever will He be our guide,
    from now until the end.

Psalm 49

¹ Come everyone and hear my words,
    come all from far and near;
Come you who live throughout the land
    and closely bend your ear.

2 Come you with blood of high estate
    and you of lowly birth;
  Come you with wealth and property
    and all the poor on earth.

3 Come listen to these words of mine
    and wisdom that is true;
  And what I know within my heart
    I'll freely share with you.

4 For I have listened for the truth
    and sought to know great things;
  And I have turned this into verse
    and music of the strings.

5 Why should I fear adversity
    and evil days ahead?
  When enemies are threatening,
    what is it I should dread?

6 Why should I be afraid of those
    who trust the wealth they gain?
  Why should I care if others boast
    of riches they obtain?

7 For they cannot redeem themselves,
    they cannot pay the price;
  There is no sacrifice to God
    that ever would suffice.

8 The ransom for a life is dear,
    the cost is far too high;
  No payment ever is enough
    despite how hard they try.

9 There is no way of cheating death,
    there will not be a stay;
  Their lives will quickly slip away
    and end up in decay.

¹⁰ For all can see the proud will die
    as sickness conquers health;
The wise and foolish pass away
    while others gain their wealth.

¹¹ Their tomb will be their dwelling place
    beneath the desert sands;
And there they will forever stay
    though once they ruled the lands.

¹² Despite their wealth and property,
    and riches they amass,
Like lowly beasts that plow the earth,
    each one of them will pass.

¹³ O this will be the fate of those
    who trust themselves alone,
As well as those who follow them,
    and all their ways condone.

¹⁴ Like sheep, they'll perish far from home
    as death leads them away;
And while they rot within their graves,
    the righteous rule the day.

¹⁵ But God will snatch me with His hand
    and lift me from the hole;
Redeeming me from death itself,
    the Lord will save my soul.

¹⁶ So do not fret when others thrive
    and when their wealth expands;
Don't worry when their riches grow
    with houses, goods and lands.

¹⁷ They cannot take these to the grave
    or keep them when they die;
There's nothing that will go with them
    when breathing their last sigh.

¹⁸ They think themselves most highly blessed
   while living out their days;
They love when others see their wealth
   and shower them with praise.

¹⁹ But they will join their ancestors
   who've gone this way before –
To be where there is darkest gloom
   and blackness evermore.

²⁰ For wealth and greatness cannot save
   or keep them in the light;
Their future is to die like beasts
   and perish in the night.

Psalm 50

¹ The Lord of lords, the Mighty God,
   the One of endless worth,
From rising to the setting sun,
   He summons all the earth.

² From Zion God has sent His light
   so all can see it shine,
A city that is beautiful,
   resplendent and divine.

³ Our God is coming with a shout,
   let earth and seas resound;
A fire goes before the Lord,
   a storm is all around.

⁴ He calls to heaven high above
   and beckons those below,
To watch Him judge His people's deeds
   and see His justice flow.

⁵ He bids His faithful people come
   to make a sacrifice –
An all-sufficient covenant
   that will for Him suffice.

⁶ The heavens overhead proclaim
    and joyfully confess,
That God is good and He is just,
    the Lord of righteousness.

⁷ Then to His people God declares,
    "Attend to what I say;
I am your God, O Israel,
    who's judging you today.

⁸ *Your sacrifices are correct,*
    I find no fault with them;
Your offerings as well suffice,
    for these I don't condemn.

⁹ *But I don't need the things you bring,*
    I have no use for goats;
I do not want your bulls or lambs
    or calves made fat on oats.

¹⁰ *For I own all the animals*
    in mountains, woods, and rills,
And all the cattle and the sheep
    upon a thousand hills.

¹¹ *I know the birds that spread their wings*
    above each mountaintop,
And all the insects in the fields
    that craw and jump and hop.

¹² *If I were weak and needed food,*
    I would not let you know;
For all within the world is mine,
    above and here below.

¹³ *I do not eat the meat of bulls*
    or feast upon their flesh;
I do not drink the blood of goats,
    for it would not refresh.

¹⁴ *The sacrifices that I want*
   are heartfelt thankfulness,
Obeying what you promise me —
   the vows that you profess.

¹⁵ *And if you call in troubled times*
   so I can hear your plea,
Then I will surely rescue you,
   and you will honor me.

¹⁶ *But wicked people — hear me well,*
   you should not quote my law,
Nor talk about my covenant,
   or on my promise draw.

¹⁷ *You hate it when I try to lead*
   and help you through Your days;
You do not listen to my words
   that guide you in my ways.

¹⁸ *You love to meet with criminals*
   and aid them in their plot;
You join adulterers in sin
   and with them cast your lot.

¹⁹ *You fill your mouth with evil words*
   that from your heart arise;
You twist your tongue into a knot
   from spreading evil lies.

²⁰ *You slander those who know you best,*
   the closest of your kin;
You bear false witness to your own,
   and by your words you sin.

²¹ *You thought that I approved these things,*
   that I was just like you;
But you were wrong, and now you're charged,
   your evil ways are through.

²² *So you who spurn me, heed my words*
    before you are destroyed;
  For when I strike, no one will come
    to save you from the void.

²³ *The only gifts that honor me*
    are gratitude and love;
  To those who do these things, I'll show
    salvation from above."

Psalm 51

¹ Have mercy on my soul, O God,
    by Your unfailing love;
  And by Your grace, blot out my sins,
    remove them from above.

² O wash away my wickedness
    and evil that's within;
  And cleanse me of my wrongful acts
    till I am free from sin.

³ For I know my iniquities
    and how I've been unkind;
  My sins are ever in the thoughts
    that occupy my mind.

⁴ Against You only have I sinned,
    transgressing in Your sight;
  And so the verdict You decree
    is justified and right.

⁵ For I was sinful at my birth,
    You knew this from the start;
  Indeed, from when I was conceived,
    I had a sinful heart.

⁶ Yet You desire faithfulness
    that wells up from the soul;
  It's there You make Your wisdom known
    that makes a person whole.

7 O purge me with pure hyssop leaves
    till like the dawn I glow;
And scrub me so I'm whiter still
    than newly fallen snow.

8 And let me hear sweet sounds of joy
    like gentle falling rain;
And let these weary bones You crushed
    rise up and dance again.

9 O God, don't look upon my sins,
    please hide them from Your face;
And wipe away my evilness
    so there is not a trace.

10 Create in me the purest heart
    so I will never stray;
Renew my spirit deep within,
    one steadfast to Your way.

11 O do not keep me far from You
    or cast my life aside;
But bid your Holy Spirit stay
    and with my soul abide.

12 Restore to me the joy that comes
    from being saved by You;
Give me a heart that does Your will,
    a spirit that is true.

13 Then I will teach transgressors, Lord,
    to follow in Your ways;
So they will turn and trust in You
    to guide them all their days.

14 O God, please save me from the guilt
    of blood upon my hands;
Then I'll proclaim Your righteousness
    and grace throughout the lands.

¹⁵ Lord, put Your words upon my lips
     and help me speak the same;
  So all will hear when I declare
     and praise Your holy name.

¹⁶ If You desired offerings,
     I'd bring a sacrifice;
  But these do not delight You, Lord,
     for You they don't suffice.

¹⁷ The only sacrifice I bring
     is my despondent heart;
  O Lord, You won't reject this gift –
     a spirit torn apart.

¹⁸ O pour Your grace on Zion, Lord,
     the city that's Your gem;
  Rebuild the grandeur of the walls
     around Jerusalem.

¹⁹ Then You'll receive burnt offerings
     by those whose hearts are right;
  And bulls upon Your altar, Lord,
     will fill You with delight.

Psalm 52

¹ Why do you boast, O mighty one,
     of evil things you do?
  For God's eternal grace and love
     will triumph over you.

² Your tongue devises wicked lies,
     destroying many lives;
  Your words cut deeply like the blades
     on razor sharpened knives.

³ You revel in your evilness,
     no goodness do you seek;
  You find enjoyment in the lies
     and hateful things you speak.

⁴ You love to curse and falsely swear,
    and in your wrongs delight;
You slander with each spoken word
    you utter out of spite.

⁵ But God will surely bring you down,
    destroying all you know;
He'll cast you from the life you live
    into the pit below.

⁶ The righteous will observe your fate
    and tremble out of fear;
Yet they will ridicule your name
    and mock you with a sneer.

⁷ They'll say you did not follow God
    but trusted in your wealth;
You put your hope in what you gained
    through subterfuge and stealth.

⁸ But I am like an olive tree
    within God's courts above,
Forever trusting in His care,
    forever in His love.

⁹ O God, for all the things You've done,
    I'll lift Your name in praise,
And tell Your people You are good,
    and trust You all my days.

Psalm 53

¹ The foolish speak from reckless hearts,
    "There is no God," they say;
Their ways are vile and fraudulent,
    and all have gone astray.

² The Lord is looking from His throne
    to see if He can find,
If anyone is seeking Him
    with all their heart and mind.

³ But all have turned from righteousness,
  corruption they extol;
There's no one who is doing good,
  no, not a single soul.

⁴ Why do the wicked eat the just
  as though consuming bread?
Why do they stay so ignorant,
  not seeking God instead?

⁵ O surely they'll be terrified,
  their hearts will shake with fear;
For God will scatter all their bones
  as shame and death draw near.

⁶ From Zion's hill salvation comes,
  let Israel delight;
When God restores His chosen ones,
  let Jacob's heart take flight.

Psalm 54

¹ O God, deliver me I pray,
  declare that I am right;
Exonerate me by Your name,
  and free me by Your might.

² Please hear my prayer to You, O God,
  and listen to my cry;
Attend to every word I speak,
  and do not pass me by.

³ For I am struck by enemies
  intent on causing strife;
These godless people make a plan
  to terminate my life.

⁴ But in Your hands You hold me, Lord,
  You guard and keep me whole;
My only help in troubled times,
  sustainer of my soul.

5 O let the evil from my foes
    return to them in kind;
Destroy them in Your faithfulness,
    their future thus consigned.

6 Then I will sacrifice to You
    a freewill offering;
And praise Your name for it is good
    as joyfully I sing.

7 O Lord, You rescued me by grace
    and freed me from my woes;
You let me look triumphantly
    on those who were my foes.

Psalm 55

1 O God, please listen to my prayer,
    the heartfelt words I cry;
Do not ignore my plea to You,
    and do not pass me by.

2 Yes, hear the things I ask of You
    for I am filled with grief;
I'm worn out from my worrying
    and desperate for relief.

3 I cringe and tremble at the threats
    from those who are my foes;
They persecute me in their hate
    and strike me with their blows.

4 My heart despairs from anguishing,
    it's paralyzed by fright;
I'm terrorized by thoughts of death
    that plague me in the night.

5 Concerns and troubles panic me
    for fear is in control;
The horror that consumes my mind
    has overwhelmed my soul.

⁶ O how I wish that I could spread
    my wings and fly away;
And like a dove I'd rise on winds
    to soar above the fray.

⁷ I'd flee to some far distant land
    within the wilderness,
A place where I could live in peace
    and settle down to rest.

⁸ I'd haste to make a shelter there,
    a dwelling safe and warm,
A place secure from blowing winds
    and every raging storm.

⁹ O Lord, confuse my enemies
    and bring their plans to shame;
For they are at the city gates
    to pillage and to maim.

¹⁰ All day and night they prowl the town,
    from shadows they appear;
With malice born of evilness,
    they choke its life with fear.

¹¹ They bring destruction to its streets,
    they knock apart its walls;
They spew forth threats and wicked lies
    so tragedy befalls.

¹² Now if insulted by my foes,
    I'd take it all in stride;
And if pursued by enemies,
    then I could run and hide.

¹³ But never did I think my friend
    would act unfaithfully –
The one who was my confidant
    and once was close to me;

¹⁴ The one who shared my deepest thoughts
    as heart-to-heart we talked;
The one who worshiped God with me
    as arm-in-arm we walked.

¹⁵ May death consume my enemies
    like fire burns up coals;
Since evil finds a dwelling place
    within their fractured souls.

¹⁶ But as for me, I call to God
    that He will hear my plea;
Then surely He will save my life –
    the Lord will rescue me.

¹⁷ For morning, noon, and through the night
    I make my heartache known;
And God attends to every cry
    and hears me when I moan.

¹⁸ Although the battle wages near
    with many who oppose,
He snatches me from every harm
    and saves me from my foes.

¹⁹ For God, Who sits enthroned above,
    and always is the same,
Will punish those who do not change
    and come to fear His name.

²⁰ But I recall my confidant,
    the one who was my friend,
Who broke a solemn covenant
    to help me to the end.

²¹ My friend spoke words as smooth as cream,
    but they were not sincere;
For though they seemed a soothing balm,
    were more like swords to fear.

22 So cast your cares upon the Lord,
   and He will guard your soul;
He will not let the righteous fall
   for He is in control.

23 O God, You bring deceivers down
   for evil things they do;
But as for me, I put my hope
   and confidence in You.

Psalm 56

1 O God, be merciful to me,
   I'm trampled by my foes;
They pummeled me in their assault
   with unrelenting blows.

2 My enemies are numerous,
   they never cease to fight;
They trample and strike out at me,
   attacking day and night.

3 But when I'm gripped by fear and dread
   and feel my life is through,
I turn again to You, O God,
   and put my trust in You.

4 And when I do, I'm not afraid,
   my soul is not alarmed;
I praise You for Your promises
   that I will not be harmed.

5 But still the wicked twist my words,
   distorting my intent;
They scheme all day to ruin me,
   which heightens my lament.

6 They gather in a hiding place
   from where they make their plans,
To watch me till they find a chance
   to crush me with their hands.

⁷ O God, because of what they've done,
    ensure that they are caught;
And in Your anger punish them
    and bring their lives to naught.

⁸ You've looked upon my misery
    and counted all my tears –
Do You not know the sum of them
    that on Your scroll appears?

⁹ For surely when I call to You
    my enemies will flee,
Because You will not leave my side,
    and always favor me.

¹⁰ O God, I love the word You give,
    I love Your awesome ways;
For this, I lift Your name on high
    and ever sing Your praise.

¹¹ And when I put my trust in You,
    there's nothing that I fear;
For what can others do to me
    as long as You are near?

¹² The vows I've made will be fulfilled
    to You, my God and King;
To thank You by a sacrifice
    will be my offering.

¹³ O Lord, You save my soul from death
    and keep me far from strife;
So all my days I'll walk with You
    within the light of life.

Psalm 57

¹ Be merciful to me, O God,
    be merciful to me;
For I take refuge in Your wings
    until the storm clouds flee.

2 I cry to You, O God Most High,
    from deep within my soul;
For You direct and guide my life
    and make my spirit whole.

3 From heaven You give victory
    so foes do not prevail;
You send Your truth and faithfulness
    and love that does not fail.

4 My enemies are all around,
    their presence stirs my fears;
Their teeth are like a row of swords,
    their tongues like sharpened spears.

5 O show Your might above us, God,
    display Your strength on high;
And let Your glory fill the earth,
    the oceans, and the sky.

6 My foes have tried to capture me
    by laying out a net;
But they themselves have fallen down
    into the trap they set.

7 My heart is ever true, O God,
    my heart is ever true;
My lips will sing the sweetest song
    to praise and worship You.

8 Awake my soul, arise with me,
    awake O harp and strings;
Together we will wake the dawn
    as all creation sings.

9 And I will worship You, O Lord,
    and thank You all my days;
Among the people everywhere,
    I'll ever sing Your praise.

¹⁰ For greater is Your faithfulness
　　than sun and stars above;
And higher still than heaven's throne
　　is Your unfailing love.

¹¹ O show Your might above us, God,
　　display Your strength on high;
And let Your glory fill the earth,
　　the oceans, and the sky.

Psalm 58

¹ Why do you rulers never make
　　a judgment that is true?
Why don't you speak with righteousness
　　so others trust in you?

² Why do you only think of hate
　　and evil you have planned,
And perpetrate your savagery
　　and violence through the land?

³ The wicked never walk in truth,
　　from birth they go awry;
They wander in their sinful ways,
　　defaming with each lie.

⁴ Their tongues are sharp and venomous
　　like poison from a snake;
Their hearts are full of spitefulness
　　that pierces like a stake.

⁵ And like a cobra that is deaf,
　　they cannot be cajoled;
No charmer's skill can ever make
　　them do what they are told.

⁶ So come, O God, remove the fangs
　　of those who prowl at night;
And break the teeth within their jaws
　　so they no longer bite.

⁷ O may the wicked disappear
    like water drains away;
  And may their bowstrings lose their pull
    and arrows go astray.

⁸ O let them be like slugs at noon
    that slowly melt to death,
  Or like a mother's stillborn child
    that never takes a breath.

⁹ For quicker than a fire flames
    when piled with thorns that burn,
  The vile will blow away like smoke,
    not ever to return.

¹⁰ The righteous will rejoice to see
    the wicked being killed;
  In victory, they'll dip their feet
    into the blood that's spilled.

¹¹ When people see the righteous blessed
    and honored for their worth,
  It's then they'll know there is a God
    who judges all the earth.

Psalm 59

¹ O Lord, my God, deliver me
    and save me from my foes;
  Defend me from their harsh attacks,
    and shield me from their blows.

² Protect me from the wicked, Lord,
    and evil they intend;
  For they have tried to spill my blood
    to bring about my end.

³ O see how they connive and plan
    and fiercely stir up strife;
  And though I have not caused offense,
    they scheme to take my life.

[4] No wrong or sin did I commit,
  yet still they flex their might;
So rouse Yourself to my defense,
  come hearken to my plight.

[5] Arise, Lord God, Almighty One,
  the God of Israel;
Arise and punish those who kill,
  and strike those who rebel.

[6] For in the evening they come out,
  like dogs they bark and howl;
Throughout the city streets they roam,
  in alleyways they prowl.

[7] Their mouths expel the vilest threats
  as sharp as any sword;
They think their insults are not heard
  no matter how untoward.

[8] But You, O Lord, are not deceived,
  You mock the words they spew –
Deriding all their evil ways
  and disregard for You.

[9] O God, because You are my strength,
  I keep You in my sight;
For like a fortress standing tall,
  You guard me by Your might.

[10] I know that Your unfailing love
  will set my soul at ease;
So I can stand triumphantly
  above my enemies.

[11] O do not slay them suddenly,
  but let their shame be known;
Uproot them by Your mighty hand
  until their spirits groan.

¹² And for the sin upon their lips
    and curses they expel,
  Let them be captured in their pride
    and trapped in lies they tell.

¹³ Destroy them in Your righteous wrath,
    and let their fate be sealed;
  Then You, the God of Israel,
    to all will be revealed.

¹⁴ For in the evening they come out,
    like dogs they bark and howl;
  About the city streets they roam,
    in alleyways they prowl.

¹⁵ They hunt for food throughout the night,
    they scavenge far and wide;
  They roar whenever hunger pangs
    have not been satisfied.

¹⁶ But in the morning I'll rejoice
    and of Your love I'll sing;
  For You're my help in troubled times,
    the One to whom I cling.

¹⁷ O God, You are my strength and shield
    Who guards me from above;
  And so I sing and praise Your name
    for Your unending love.

Psalm 60

¹ O God, You have rejected us
    and kept us far from You;
  Too long You've let Your anger burn
    so turn to us anew.

² For You have torn and rocked the world
    and caused the earth to sink;
  So come and heal this broken land
    that's standing on the brink.

³ You filled our lives with suffering
    and trials without relief;
You served us bitter wine to drink
    that staggered us with grief.

⁴ But as for those who fear Your name,
    You raise a banner high;
So all may see and know Your truth
    and to Your colors fly.

⁵ So come, O Lord, deliver us
    by strength of Your right hand;
Protect those whom You dearly love
    who dwell within Your land.

⁶ For in the temple You once said,
    "I give to you this oath:
That I will portion Shechem's land
    and parcel out Succoth.

⁷ *For Gilead belongs to me,*
    Manasseh's my delight;
I've Judah's scepter for my rule
    and Ephraim as my might.

⁸ *But Moab is my washing bowl,*
    and Edom feels my shoe;
While over Philistia's tribes
    I'll shout with strength anew."

⁹ O who will go before me, Lord,
    to fortify my cause?
And who will guide me on the way
    that leads to Edom's walls?

¹⁰ O Lord, have You rejected us?
    Do You not hear our pleas?
Will You not help our armies fight
    against our enemies?

¹¹ O help us in the battle, Lord,
    to crush those we oppose;
For human help has little worth
    and won't defeat our foes.

¹² For You give us the victory
    and help us win the war;
You tread upon our enemy
    to make our triumph sure.

Psalm 61

¹ O hear my cry to You, O God,
    my soul is in despair;
Please know me in my neediness
    and listen to my prayer.

² I call to You from far away,
    my spirit is distressed;
Direct me to that highest rock
    where I can find my rest.

³ For You have been my hideaway,
    a tower standing tall,
A fortress from my enemies,
    a harbor in a squall.

⁴ I long to live within Your care
    so I can safely sleep,
While sheltered underneath Your wings,
    secure within Your keep.

⁵ For You, O God, have heard my vows,
    You know what I proclaim;
You've given me the blessings due
    to those who fear Your name.

⁶ Extend the king's longevity,
    sustain him by Your might;
Increase his years so he may live
    and dwell within Your sight.

7 O may the king forever reign
  and in Your presence stand,
 Held by Your love and faithfulness
  and sheltered by Your hand.

8 Then I will lift Your name, O God,
  and ever sing Your praise,
 While I fulfill my vows to You
  and keep them all my days.

Psalm 62

1 My soul finds rest in God alone
  because of grace He shows;
 My hope and rescue come from Him,
  for I'm the one He chose.

2 In God I have a solid rock,
  a tower without peer,
 A fortress keeping me secure
  so I need never fear.

3 How long will foes descend on me
  to shatter my defense?
 For I am like a leaning wall,
  a worn and broken fence.

4 My adversaries plan my fall,
  with lies they lay a snare;
 They utter blessings with their mouths
  while inwardly they swear.

5 Await my soul, and do not speak,
  be quiet now, be stilled;
 Take rest and comfort in the Lord,
  and find your hope fulfilled.

6 In God I have a solid rock,
  a tower without peer,
 A fortress keeping me secure
  so I need never fear.

⁷ On God my hope and glory rests,
    in Him my faith resides;
For He's my shelter and my strength,
    a refuge that provides.

⁸ So give your heart to God alone,
    to Him commit your trust;
For God's a refuge for the soul
    because He's good and just.

⁹ The rich and poor are but a breath,
    inadequate and frail,
Together not a puff of smoke
    if weighed upon a scale.

¹⁰ So do not trust in stolen goods,
    or you will hope in vain;
And even if a windfall comes,
    don't trust upon your gain.

¹¹ For God has spoken by His word
    and made it clearly known,
That strength and power come from Him,
    they're His and His alone.

¹² But love is also from the Lord,
    His grace will see us through;
For He rewards us for our deeds
    and all we say and do.

Psalm 63

¹ O God, my God, my soul is parched
    and dearly thirsts for You;
It seeks You like the desert craves
    the dampness of the dew.

² I've seen You in the temple courts,
    which filled me with delight;
I've looked upon Your awesome strength
    and glory of Your might.

3 The life You've given me is dear,
    yet better is Your love;
  So may the blessings from my lips
    arise to You above.

4 And all my days I'll give You thanks
    and praise You through the lands;
  I'll glorify and honor You
    by lifting up my hands.

5 By this my soul is satisfied,
    through this it is fulfilled;
  My lips will ever sing to You
    with joy that won't be stilled.

6 I'll think of You while in my bed
    when darkness veils the light;
  I'll meditate on You, O God,
    throughout the still of night.

7 Because You are my strength and help,
    my spirit gladly sings,
  Secure and safe beneath the shield
    and shadow of Your wings.

8 My soul clings fast to You, O God,
    protected it will stand;
  You shelter me within Your arms,
    upheld by Your right hand.

9 But those who seek to take my life
    with blows that strike me down,
  Will fall into a gaping pit
    and perish in the ground.

10 Because they seek to murder me,
    they'll perish by the sword;
  Their flesh will be the food of wolves,
    their death a just reward.

¹¹ O let the righteous and the king
    rejoice and give God praise;
For He will still the liars' mouths
    and end their lying ways.

Psalm 64

¹ O God, please listen to my prayer,
    the depth of my complaint;
Defend me from my enemies
    who strike without restraint.

² Protect me from conspiracies,
    the wicked and their plans;
Defend me from their sinful ways
    and clutches of their hands.

³ The wicked hone their evil tongues
    like swords before a fight;
They aim their cruel and bitter words
    like bowstrings pulled back tight.

⁴ The wicked crouch in hideaways
    when victims venture near;
Then quickly strike with shameless lies
    because they have no fear.

⁵ The wicked hatch their evil plots
    while they are lying low;
And as they set their traps they say,
    "There's no one who will know."

⁶ The wicked plot injustices
    and boast how they are smart;
O surely evil is the mind
    and devious the heart.

⁷ The wicked though will not succeed
    for God is swift to act;
He shoots His arrows perfectly,
    His aiming is exact.

8 The wicked thus will be condemned
    for every word they voice;
Their lives will be disdained by all
    who see them and rejoice.

9 Then people everywhere will fear
    the power of God's hand;
They'll contemplate His mighty works
    and try to understand.

10 The righteous will exalt the Lord
    and trust Him all their days;
With grateful tongues they'll worship Him
    with joyful songs of praise.

Psalm 65

1 O God, we will fulfill our word
    to give You all our praise;
We'll worship You on Zion's hill
    both now and all our days.

2 You hear us when we call to You
    and answer when we pray;
O surely all who live on earth
    will come to You one day.

3 You overwhelm us by Your grace,
    forgiving every sin;
You pardon wicked words and deeds
    and evilness within.

4 How happy to be known by You
    and held in Your embrace;
You fill us from the bounty stored
    within Your holy place.

5 With awesome deeds You answer us,
    responding to our pleas;
O righteous God, You are the hope
    of earth and farthest seas.

⁶ You formed the mountains by Your hands,
    each peak and soaring height;
You filled them with Your majesty
    so all would see Your might.

⁷ You stilled the thunder of the seas,
    the pounding waves that roar;
You calmed the nations of their rage
    and turbulence of war.

⁸ Your wonders fill the earth with awe,
    the people stand amazed;
From morning dawn to eventide,
    sweet songs of joy are raised.

⁹ You lovingly attend the land,
    You cover it with rain;
You fill the springs and warm the ground
    producing fields of grain.

¹⁰ You soak the furrows of the fields,
    You level all the tops;
You soften them with gentle mist
    and bless the autumn crops.

¹¹ You crown the year with oats and wheat
    with golden heads that glow;
You heap the carts at harvest time
    until they overflow.

¹² Through You, O God, each grassy field
    abundantly is blessed;
The dales are clothed in thankfulness,
    with joy the hills are dressed.

¹³ And so the meadows packed with flocks
    and valleys thick with grain,
Will raise their voices joyfully,
    and sing a sweet refrain.

Psalm 66

¹ Prepare to lift your voices high,
    all people of the earth;
Shout joyfully to God above,
    the One of greatest worth.

² O sing the glory of His name
    and His amazing ways;
O sing a song that glorifies
    and gives Him all your praise.

³ And say to God, *"How wonderful*
    Your awesome acts appear;
Your power overwhelms Your foes
    and grips their hearts with fear.

⁴ *The people of the earth bow down*
    with worship and acclaim;
They lift their voices as they sing
    the praises of Your name."

⁵ So come and see the works of God,
    His wonders from above;
Come look upon His awesome deeds
    that witness to His love.

⁶ He turned the seas to solid ground,
    the waters into land;
He led His people safely through,
    so praise His mighty hand.

⁷ He rules the nations by His strength
    and keeps them in His sight;
Let no one turn against the Lord
    by challenging His might.

⁸ So come now people, bless our God
    with happy voices raised;
And let the joyous sound go forth
    so He'll be ever praised.

⁹ For He preserves and shelters us
    to keep our souls secure;
He does not let us trip and fall
    but makes our footing sure.

¹⁰ O God, You sorely tested us,
    to try us was Your aim,
Like silver cleansed and purified
    within the furnace flame.

¹¹ You let us walk into a trap
    where we were tied and bound;
You laid a burden on our backs
    that crushed us to the ground.

¹² You let our foes ride over us,
    we went through flood and blaze;
But then You brought us to a place
    of blessings for our days.

¹³ So I will come into Your house
    to make an offering;
My solemn vows are what I give,
    the sacrifice I bring.

¹⁴ And I will keep my promises,
    the pledges that I made,
The vows I swore in troubled times
    when I was sore afraid.

¹⁵ I'll freely make a sacrifice,
    an offering of rams,
Burnt offerings of animals –
    of fatted goats and lambs.

¹⁶ Let those who fear and honor God
    come listen to my voice;
I'll tell of what He's done for me
    that makes my soul rejoice.

¹⁷ I cried aloud for God to hear
　　and not to pass me by;
　I worshipped Him with lifted voice
　　and praised His name on high.

¹⁸ Now if I had ignored my wrongs
　　and wickedness within,
　Then God would not have heard me call
　　because He knows my sin.

¹⁹ But God has listened to my pleas
　　because of how He cares;
　Attentive to the things I need,
　　He surely hears my prayers.

²⁰ So praise and blessings be to God,
　　exalted high above;
　For He has not ignored my prayer
　　or kept me from His love.

Psalm 67

¹ O God, be gracious to our souls
　　and bless us all our days;
　Allow Your face to shine on us
　　and keep us in Your gaze.

² May every blessing You pour out
　　be known throughout the land;
　So all will see the saving grace
　　delivered by Your hand.

³ O may the people praise You, God,
　　and glorify Your name;
　May all the people praise You now
　　with honor and acclaim.

⁴ May people shout and sing for joy
　　to magnify Your worth;
　For You adjudge with equity
　　and guide those here on earth.

⁵ O may the people praise You, God,
and glorify Your name;
May all the people praise You now
with honor and acclaim.

⁶ The land has borne a bumper crop
and yielded up its best;
For You, our God, provided it
so we are greatly blessed.

⁷ Because You richly fill our lives
and bless us every day,
May people fear and honor You
and follow in Your way.

Psalm 68

¹ May God arise against His foes
and meet them with His might;
May He attack and scatter them
so they no longer fight.

² Like wax is melted by a blaze
and smoke fades in the sky,
May God disperse and crush the vile
and plague them till they die.

³ The righteous will be jubilant
and lift a happy voice;
They'll sing a song unto the Lord
and gratefully rejoice.

⁴ O sing to God who rides on clouds,
and glorify His name;
For He is Lord, so honor Him
with worship and acclaim.

⁵ Within His temple God displays
His justice and His care;
He tends to widows in distress
and orphans in despair.

⁶ God sets the captives free again
    and brings the lonely home;
But rebels will be driven out
    to deserts where they'll roam.

⁷ O Lord, You led Your people through
    the barren wilderness;
Your presence went before the tribes,
    ensuring their success.

⁸ The earth convulsed in front of You,
    the heavens burst with rain,
Before the God of Israel
    on Sinai's arid plain.

⁹ You poured down showers from above
    by reaching our Your hand,
Refreshing and restoring life
    within a weary land.

¹⁰ You led Your people to a place
    where they could live secure;
You fed them by Your kindliness
    and satisfied the poor.

¹¹ The Lord declared by his command
    the things that would appear;
While scores of women spread the news
    so everyone would hear:

¹² *"Great kings and armies turn and run*
    and seek to get away;
The women portion out the wealth,
    the spoils of the day.

¹³ *And while some sleep, the others count*
    the plundered goods they hold —
White doves with silver-plated wings
    and feathers made of gold."

¹⁴ O when the Lord dispersed the kings,
   He scattered them below,
As though a storm on Zalmon's peak
   was blowing flakes of snow.

¹⁵ Mount Bashan is magnificent,
   resplendent in the light,
A rugged mountain soaring high,
   evoking strength and might.

¹⁶ So why, Mount Bashan, do you gaze
   and look with such distain,
Upon the hill that God has made,
   the place from which He'll reign.

¹⁷ With chariots more numerous
   than any foe can face,
The Lord comes out of Sinai's plains
   to dwell within His place.

¹⁸ The Lord goes upward to the heights
   with captives in His hand;
He takes the tribute offered Him
   from rebels in the land.

¹⁹ So glory be to God above,
   our Savior whom we praise,
Who gives us life and bears for us
   the burden of our days.

²⁰ The Lord Our God, the One who saves,
   provides us life and breath;
From Him comes our deliverance
   and our escape from death.

²¹ For God will surely crush the heads
   of those who are His foes,
To punish them for all their sins –
   the source of many woes.

²² God said, *"I'll bring the wicked back*
    from Bashan where they hide;
  I'll bring them from the ocean depths,
    from seas below the tide.

²³ *And you, my people, will prevail,*
    the wicked won't be spared;
  Your feet will trample in their blood,
    your dogs will have their share."

²⁴ Then God's procession will arrive
    while everyone awaits;
  And God, my King, will show the way
    into His temple gates.

²⁵ First singers, then musicians come,
    the retinue convenes;
  And in their midst young women dance
    and play their tambourines.

²⁶ So come now sing and praise the Lord
    wherever you may dwell;
  Exalt Him as He passes by,
    O praise Him Israel.

²⁷ The tribe of Benjamin will lead
    with princes in their throng;
  While Zebulun and Naphtali
    and Judah trail along.

²⁸ So call upon Your power, God,
    disclose Your strength and might;
  Reveal to us the things You've done,
    O bring them now to light.

²⁹ Your temple in Jerusalem
    is lovely to behold;
  Great kings and princes seeing it
    will bring You gifts of gold.

30 But strike the nation on the Nile,
    that beast among the reeds;
And though they bring You silver bars,
    destroy them for their deeds.

31 For surely the Egyptians come
    with tribute from their lands;
And even those who live in Cush,
    to God will raise their hands.

32 So come now sing sweet songs to God,
    you kingdoms of the earth;
And with your voices praise the Lord,
    the One of endless worth.

33 O sing to Him who rides on clouds
    across the ancient skies,
Who thunders with a mighty roar
    that never fades or dies.

34 Proclaim to all the strength of God,
    declare His majesty,
The One who governs Israel
    with power all can see.

35 For God is awesome in His courts,
    His people He's restored;
The God of Israel gives strength,
    so praise and bless the Lord.

Psalm 69

1 God, save me from the rising tide
    that slowly pulls me down;
The waters are above my neck,
    and I'm about to drown.

2 I'm sinking in the miry deep
    without a place to stand;
I'm threatened by the growing flood
    and far away from land.

³ I'm weary from my cries for help,
   my throat is parched and scored;
I'm blinded and my eyes grow dim
   from waiting for You, Lord.

⁴ My foes are far more numerous
   than hairs upon my head;
They make me yield what's rightly mine
   and want to see me dead.

⁵ O God, You know my foolishness,
   my folly and my shame;
The wrongs I've done I cannot hide,
   I've only me to blame.

⁶ Almighty God of Israel,
   don't let the things I do,
Dishonor or embarrass those
   who put their hope in You.

⁷ I'm scorned and suffer mockery
   because I bear Your name;
My face is covered with disgrace,
   I'm overcome with shame.

⁸ I'm cut off from my family,
   estranged from everyone;
I'm spurned by all my relatives
   with no place left to run.

⁹ Because I'm zealous for Your house
   and faithful to Your name,
I take the insults meant for You,
   receiving all the blame.

¹⁰ I'm criticized for shedding tears,
   I'm censured when I fast;
Whenever I am seeking You,
   I'm chided and harassed.

[11] And when I'm mourning in my soul
    with sackcloth as my gown,
The wicked treat me with disdain
    and scorn me through the town.

[12] And those who gossip at the gate
    have mocked me to the throng;
While drunkards taunt me with their words
    and slander me with song.

[13] So when I pray to You, O Lord,
    for favor from above,
Please answer me with saving grace
    and Your unfailing love.

[14] O rescue me from sinking mud,
    and do not let me drown;
Deliver me from every foe
    who tries to pull me down.

[15] Don't let me trip before the flood
    or slip beneath a wave;
Don't let me sink below the tide
    or fall into the grave.

[16] Don't close Your ears, but answer me,
    because Your love is fair;
O by Your steadfast mercy, Lord,
    respond to my despair.

[17] Don't hide Your countenance from me,
    don't turn and look away;
Come quickly for I'm suffering
    and need Your help today.

[18] Don't keep Your presence far from me,
    come near and save my soul;
Deliver me from every foe,
    redeem and make me whole.

19 For You know my dishonor, Lord,
    You watch the way I'm shamed;
You see me humbled by my foes
    and hear how I'm defamed.

20 Their taunts and insults crush my heart
    till I can only groan;
I look for comfort everywhere,
    but I am all alone.

21 They sprinkle poison in my food
    when I am needing meat;
They give me vinegar to drink
    when thirsting from the heat.

22 So may their table be a trap
    to catch them unaware;
May every good thing they possess
    become for them a snare.

23 May all their eyes grow dark as night
    until they cannot see;
May they have weak and twisted backs
    and suffer endlessly.

24 May You pour out Your wrath and rage
    to crush them like the tide;
O may Your anger overtake
    and catch them in their stride.

25 May all their camps be desolate,
    may none of them survive;
And may their tents stand silently
    with no one left alive.

26 For they oppress those You Yourself
    have stricken by Your hand;
They talk about the sufferings
    of those You reprimand.

²⁷ So keep a record of their guilt
     and their iniquity;
Don't save them with the righteous, Lord,
     and do not set them free.

²⁸ Expunge them from the book of life,
     return them to the dust;
O do not list them with Your own –
     the righteous and the just.

²⁹ Because I'm sick from suffering,
     in anguish and despair,
Protect me by Your grace, O God,
     and keep me in Your care.

³⁰ O I will sing a song to God
     that glorifies His name;
I'll honor Him with gratitude,
     His glory to proclaim.

³¹ For praise and worship pleases God,
     He hears it and approves,
Much more than sin-guilt offerings
     of bulls with cloven hooves.

³² And all who seek the Lord will come,
     the humble and the poor;
And all their hearts will be revived
     and filled with hope once more.

³³ The Lord attends to those in chains,
     the captives and oppressed;
He won't forget the ones He loves
     who need a place of rest.

³⁴ So let the heavens and the earth
     lift up His name in praise;
And let the seas and all therein
     exalt Him all their days.

³⁵ For Zion will be saved by God,
 and Judah's walls repaired;
His people will establish roots
 in places He prepared.

³⁶ Their offspring will inherit it
 because they love the Lord;
And they will live within the land
 that God Himself restored.

Psalm 70

¹ O God, make haste and rescue me
 and do not pass me by;
Be merciful and help me, Lord,
 come quickly and draw nigh.

² May those who seek to take my life
 be thoroughly ashamed;
And those who want to ruin me
 be turned back and defamed.

³ May those who mock and laugh at me
 with wickedness and scorn,
Be shamed and humbled in defeat,
 embarrassed, and forlorn.

⁴ But those who seek to know You, Lord,
 and in Your love rejoice,
May they declare *"The Lord is great,"*
 together with one voice.

⁵ O I am weak and needy, Lord,
 so think of me today;
Come quickly and deliver me,
 make haste now don't delay.

Psalm 71

1 O Lord, I've always looked to You
   to be my hiding place;
So never let me be ashamed,
   and shield me from disgrace.

2 Lord, save me by Your righteousness,
   deliver me I pray;
O listen when I cry to You,
   and keep me safe today.

3 Lord, be a shelter for my soul,
   a refuge when I knock,
A tower and a mighty keep,
   a fortress and a rock.

4 Lord, snatch me from my enemies,
   from cruel and wicked hands;
Deliver me from those who act
   with vile and evil plans.

5 O Lord, You are my only hope,
   my trust throughout the years;
In You alone I put my faith
   to soothe my angst and fears.

6 Lord, from my birth I've leaned on You,
   it's You who gave me breath;
And with the strength that comes from You,
   I'll praise You till my death.

7 My life is deemed remarkable
   by those who look and see;
For You have kept me safe from harm
   and always cared for me.

8 O Lord, I lift my voice in praise
   and worship You in song,
Declaring your magnificence
   and glory all day long.

⁹ Although my days are growing short,
    and I am old and drawn,
  Do not forsake or leave me, Lord,
    like one whose hope is gone.

¹⁰ My enemies speak words of hate
    from spirits born of strife;
  They make their plans, then lie in wait
    to take away my life.

¹¹ And when they look at me they say,
    "God's nowhere to be seen,
  So let's pursue and seize him now
    since none will intervene."

¹² O God, do not be distant now,
    but come to me I pray;
  Be swift to act in my defense
    before I pass away.

¹³ May all my adversaries fall
    in scandal and disgrace;
  May those who want to do me harm
    wear shame upon their face.

¹⁴ Yet I will always hope in You,
    and in my heart rejoice;
  I'll worship You with all my strength
    and praise You with my voice.

¹⁵ O I will tell about Your works
    and acts of righteousness;
  Indeed, I cannot count the sum
    of all the ways You bless.

¹⁶ And I'll proclaim to everyone
    the justice You have shown,
  Announcing every mighty work
    that comes from You alone.

¹⁷ For You have tutored me, O God,
   and taught me from my youth;
And to this day I praise Your deeds
   and wonders of Your truth.

¹⁸ So even though I'm old and gray,
   please keep me in Your sight;
So I can educate the young
   about Your strength and might.

¹⁹ Your righteousness is boundless, Lord,
   it reaches to the skies;
For many awesome things You've done,
   there's none as grand and wise.

²⁰ Although You've sent me troubles, Lord,
   and many days of pain,
Your hand will lift me from the grave
   to give me life again.

²¹ And You will make me great once more
   with accolades anew;
You'll comfort me within Your arms
   and hold me close to You.

²² I'll thank You for Your faithfulness
   with lyre, harp and string;
O Holy One of Israel,
   Your praises I will sing.

²³ My lips will overflow with joy
   when singing of Your praise;
For You have saved me by Your grace
   and set my heart ablaze.

²⁴ O I'll declare Your righteousness
   from morning to the night;
For those who've tried to injure me
   are shamed and put to flight.

Psalm 72

[1] O God, confer Your righteousness
    upon the royal heir;
Let justice be his sovereign robe,
    and truth his crown to wear.

[2] The king will judge with equity
    the people You hold dear,
Dispensing justice to the poor
    and those who live in fear.

[3] From rivers born in mountain springs,
    prosperity will flow;
The hills will bloom with peace and truth,
    and righteousness will grow.

[4] The king will aid the destitute
    and put their foes to flight;
He'll save the children of the poor
    and guard them by his might.

[5] O God, may You be glorified
    as long as stars endure,
Until the sun and moon grow dark,
    for ages evermore.

[6] And may the king be like the rain
    that falls upon a field,
A shower watering the earth,
    which offers up its yield.

[7] May righteousness and justice bloom
    and flourish like a rose;
May peace abound throughout the land
    as long as moonlight glows.

[8] O may the king extend his rule
    from sea to shining sea,
From where the wide Euphrates flows
    beyond where one can flee.

⁹ May desert tribes bow down to him
    and fall upon their knees;
And may his enemies be tossed
    like dust before the breeze.

¹⁰ May kings of Tarshish bring their gifts
    from far and distant shores;
May Sheba's king and Seba's prince
    pay tribute from their stores.

¹¹ May lords submit when he is near
    by humbly bowing down;
May nations live to serve the king,
    the one who wears the crown.

¹² The king will rescue those in need,
    responding to their call;
And he will aid the destitute,
    providing help to all.

¹³ The king has pity on the weak,
    the needy and enslaved;
And he will surely rescue them
    so many lives are saved.

¹⁴ The king will snatch them from their foes
    and save them from the fight;
For every life and drop of blood
    is precious in his sight.

¹⁵ May gold from Sheba come to him,
    may he be well and strong;
May people ever pray for him
    and bless him all day long.

¹⁶ May fields produce a grain that's rich,
    and trees yield fruit that's sweet;
May cities thrive like Lebanon
    and bloom like golden wheat.

^{17} And may his name be ever known,
    enduring like the sun;
  May nations all be blessed through him
    and honor what he's done.

^{18} So praise be to the Lord above,
    the God above all kings,
  The Holy One of Israel,
    the God who does great things.

^{19} Yes, blessings to the name of God,
    forever and again;
  And may His glory fill the earth,
    so Amen and Amen.

Psalm 73

^{1} The Lord is good to Israel,
    a nation set apart;
  He's faithful to the virtuous,
    the pure in mind and heart.

^{2} But as for me, I nearly slipped
    and floundered in the dust;
  I wavered in my faithfulness,
    my confidence and trust.

^{3} For I saw how the wicked thrived
    by subterfuge and stealth;
  I envied their prosperity
    and how they gathered wealth.

^{4} The wicked seem to be untouched
    by any ill or wrong;
  Their bodies feel no pain till death,
    they're always fit and strong.

^{5} The wicked do not suffer trials
    or grief that mortals bear;
  They are not plagued by human woes
    or driven to despair.

⁶ The wicked wear a covering
    of arrogance and pride;
They clothe themselves with violence,
    reflecting what's inside.

⁷ The wicked harbor sinful hearts
    that feed their wrongful plans;
They nurture vile and evil thoughts
    and act with unclean hands.

⁸ The wicked scoff at those they see
    with spite and hatefulness;
And in their haughty spirits plot
    to threaten and oppress.

⁹ The wicked speak against the Lord,
    disparaging His name;
They raise their voices far and wide
    to boast about their fame.

¹⁰ The wicked have their followers
    whose lives are led astray;
And even those who fear the Lord
    have trusted what they say.

¹¹ The wicked boast, *"How can God know*
    about the things we do?
Does God observe the way we live
    or if we've been untrue?"

¹² The wicked live a carefree life
    that keeps their minds at peace;
They overflow with wealth and goods
    that constantly increase.

¹³ So was I wise to guard my heart?
    Did I know any gain?
Or was my time of innocence
    mere folly and in vain?

¹⁴ For I have suffered endlessly
    through sickness and malaise;
  I'm punished when the morning breaks
    and plagued through endless days.

¹⁵ But if I said, *"I'll speak like those
    with evil on their tongue,"*
  Then I would shame Your people, Lord,
    the elders and the young.

¹⁶ I saw the wicked have success
    and grieved when they prevailed;
  I felt discouraged and confused,
    my understanding failed.

¹⁷ But then Your temple beckoned me
    to enter through its gate;
  And when inside Your Holy place,
    at last I knew their fate.

¹⁸ For You will make the wicked slip
    and fall upon the ground;
  Your hand will cast them in the pit
    till none of them are found.

¹⁹ How swiftly are their lives destroyed,
    how quickly they are spent;
  How suddenly their ending comes,
    with no time to lament.

²⁰ Like dreams that slowly melt away
    when daylight greets the morn,
  When You arise, the wicked fade,
    for You despise their form.

²¹ Yet when I did not understand
    that You were in control,
  My spirit was embittered, Lord,
    I grieved within my soul.

²² My senses all abandoned me,
    my apprehension grew;
I acted like a savage beast
    and raged in front of You.

²³ Yet nonetheless I have not strayed
    as near to You I stand;
You always draw and keep me close
    while holding my right hand.

²⁴ You counsel and direct my steps
    and guide me like a friend,
Receiving me to glory, Lord,
    when I have reached my end.

²⁵ For whom in heaven do I have?
    There's no one else but You.
There's nothing that I want on earth –
    it's You I'm looking to.

²⁶ And though my hope and courage fail
    and flesh be torn apart,
Forever You're my portion, Lord,
    the strength that girds my heart.

²⁷ For every soul will perish, Lord,
    who lives apart from You;
You'll bring destruction on the vile,
    the faithless and untrue.

²⁸ But as for me, it's good, O Lord,
    to know Your sweet embrace,
To be protected by Your arms,
    and tell about Your grace.

Psalm 74

¹ God, why have you rejected us
    and cast us from Your keep?
Why does Your anger burn so long
    on those who are Your sheep?

2 Remember, God, Your chosen ones –
   redeemed to be Your own;
   Recall Mount Zion where You dwelled
   in glory on Your throne.

3 O see Your sanctuary, Lord,
   and how it's been debased,
   Demolished by Your enemies,
   in ruins and defaced.

4 Come see Your holy place, O Lord,
   where once Your name was praised;
   Your foes defiled it with their words
   and evil signs they raised.

5 They came with axes lifted up
   and swinging in the breeze,
   As if preparing to cut down
   a mighty stand of trees.

6 They swung their hatchets savagely,
   destroying what they could;
   They chopped the sculpted paneling
   and carvings made of wood.

7 They wrecked Your sanctuary, God,
   and burned it to the ground;
   They sullied, then laid waste to it
   until no trace was found.

8 They sought to cause Your people harm
   and crush them by their hand;
   They burned each place where once Your name
   was worshiped in the land.

9 And yet we see no signs from You,
   no prophet speaking straight;
   We do not know what will occur
   or how long we must wait.

^{10} How long, O God, will You be mocked?
How long will this go on?
How long will foes revile Your name?
How long until they're gone?

^{11} How long will You withhold Your hand
and keep it at Your side?
How long until Your right hand strikes
and kills them in their stride?

^{12} O God, You are my King from old,
the One of greatest worth,
Who works salvation everywhere,
within and through the earth.

^{13} God, it was You who split the sea
and held it in Your hand;
You smashed the great Leviathan
and tossed it on the land.

^{14} God, it was You who crushed its head –
that monster of the deep,
And fed its body to the birds
like grains of ripened wheat.

^{15} God, it was You who opened springs
and torrents with a blow,
Who dried up rivers at their source
to stem their mighty flow.

^{16} God, it was You who made the day
and called the darkness night,
Who formed the sun, and placed the moon
and each celestial light.

^{17} God, it was You who marked the earth
and mapped it with a string,
Who made the winter and the fall,
the summertime and spring.

¹⁸ O Lord, do not forget the slurs
　　Your enemies proclaim;
　Remember every foolish tongue
　　that speaks against Your name.

¹⁹ O do not let Your precious dove
　　be eaten by the hawk;
　Do not forget Your people's plight,
　　the hardship of their walk.

²⁰ Do not forsake Your covenant
　　or stay Your mighty hand;
　As forces dark and violent
　　now occupy the land.

²¹ Do not allow the beaten down
　　to turn back in disgrace;
　But let the poor rejoice again
　　and praise You for Your grace.

²² Arise, O God, and don't delay,
　　defend Your righteous cause;
　Remember those who mock Your name
　　and disobey Your laws.

²³ Do not forget Your enemies
　　and their defiant roar;
　Do not ignore the shouts of foes
　　whose conduct You abhor.

Psalm 75

¹ O God, we give our thanks to You
　　for always being near;
　We tell about Your wondrous deeds
　　so all the earth will hear.

² Your words declare, *"I set the time,*
　　the choice belongs to me;
　It's I who will select the place
　　to judge with equity.

³ *And when the earth is rocked by quakes,*
  and people shake and fall,
 It's I who hold the pillars strong,
  securing one and all.

⁴ *Now to the proud, I say these words,*
  'Make no more boasts today;'
 And to the wicked, I advise,
  'Don't tout your prideful way.'

⁵ *For none should speak against the things*
  that I alone prepared,
 Nor denigrate in arrogance
  the words that I've declared."

⁶ O righteous judgments do not come
  from any mortal hand;
 There's no one from the east or west
  who gives a just command.

⁷ For God alone is judge of all
  and rules by right decree,
 Condemning some for what they've done,
  while setting others free.

⁸ God pours His righteous anger out
  like wine into a cup;
 The wicked drink it to its dregs,
  compelled to lap it up.

⁹ But as for me, I'll raise my voice
  and ever sing His praise;
 My soul will worship Jacob's God
  for now and all my days.

¹⁰ The Lord will strike the wicked down
  and make their power cease;
 But He will lift the righteous up
  and see their strength increase.

Psalm 76

¹ In Judah God is known to all,
    His name's on every tongue;
In Israel He is revered
    by elders and the young.

² In Salem God has made a home
    to be a place of rest;
In Zion God comes down to dwell
    with those whom He has blessed.

³ It's there He broke the shields and swords,
    and weapons kept in store;
He snapped the arrows and the bows
    that fighters take to war.

⁴ O God, You are more glorious
    than starry host aflame,
Your splendor more magnificent
    than hills alive with game.

⁵ O God, You caused Your valiant foes
    to sleep their final sleep;
Their strength could not prevent their fall,
    their hands were far too weak.

⁶ O God of Jacob, at Your word,
    their horses' neighs were hushed;
And at Your piercing battle cry,
    their warriors were crushed.

⁷ O God, You're held in awe by those
    who fear You and obey;
For none can bear Your anger, Lord,
    or stand against Your way.

⁸ From heaven You announced Your word
    so all would know Your will;
Then everyone was filled with awe,
    and all the earth was still.

⁹ It's then You rose to judge the world
    and issue Your command,
  To save the beaten and oppressed,
    the helpless in the land.

¹⁰ O God, Your wrath rebukes the vile,
    and people give You praise;
  So those who live will be restrained
    and spurn their evil ways.

¹¹ So everyone now make Your vows
    and keep them to the Lord;
  O bring to Him, the One who's feared,
    the bounty you have stored.

¹² God humbles those who rule the earth
    and breaks their selfish pride;
  He terrifies the mighty kings
    and princes far and wide.

Psalm 77

¹ O God, I lift my plea to You
    and cry that You will hear;
  I raise my voice in helplessness
    and ask that You draw near.

² I seek You in my suffering,
    in misery untold;
  At night I raise my hands in prayer
    but cannot be consoled.

³ For when I think of You, O God,
    I groan without restraint;
  And when I try to meditate,
    my weary soul grows faint.

⁴ You keep my eyes from closing, Lord,
    my tired bones grow weak;
  My soul is troubled deep within,
    I find no words to speak.

⁵ My thoughts are turning to the past,
    to days and years gone by;
And when I think of long ago,
    I feel my spirit sigh.

⁶ The memories that come to me
    are like a song at night;
I ponder them within my heart
    and think about my plight.

⁷ Will God forever turn from me?
    Will He forsake my life?
Will He no longer look on me
    when I am facing strife?

⁸ Has God withheld His love from me
    and caused His grace to end?
And on His word and promises,
    can I no more depend?

⁹ Has God stopped being kind to me
    and let His mercy cease?
Has His compassion been withheld?
    His anger trumped His peace?

¹⁰ It deeply grieves me in my soul
    and leaves my mind confused,
To think that God's right hand has changed
    and won't again be used.

¹¹ O Lord, I contemplate Your works
    and deeds from ancient days,
The miracles and things You did,
    the marvel of Your ways.

¹² I think about Your awesome feats
    and all that You have made;
I meditate upon Your acts
    and wonders You've displayed.

¹³ For You alone are holy, Lord,
    there's none who is so fair;
There is no god as great as You,
    no one who can compare.

¹⁴ O God, You make the miracles
    that happen every day;
You let the people see Your strength
    and power of Your way.

¹⁵ You reached Your arm and saved the lives
    of those whom You esteemed,
So Jacob's heirs would be set free,
    and Joseph's seed redeemed.

¹⁶ O God, the waters saw You move
    and churned as in a fit;
With shuddering and writhing fear,
    the deepest oceans split.

¹⁷ With crashing bursts, the clouds were pierced,
    the rain poured from the sky;
The lightning flashed and bounced about
    like arrows shooting high.

¹⁸ Your thunder sounded near and far,
    it traveled through the air;
It caused the earth to rock and shake
    and tremble everywhere.

¹⁹ The way You set was through the deep
    where waters rise and fall;
Yet none could see Your footprints, Lord,
    You left no trace at all.

²⁰ By Moses hand and Aaron's rod,
    Your flock passed through the sea;
Yet all the while You led the way
    and guided carefully.

Psalm 78

1 Come people now from east and west
    and lands both north and south;
Come hear the wisdom in the words
    as spoken from my mouth.

2 My tongue will speak in parables,
    of things that once were told,
Of riddles and of mysteries
    that are from days of old.

3 Yes, I'll pass on what we have learned,
    the knowledge we have gained,
The things our elders have revealed,
    and how they were explained.

4 For we must tell of God's great strength
    to those who've yet to come,
Recounting all the miracles
    and wonders He has done.

5 The Lord gave Jacob His decrees,
    His law to Israel,
Commanding elders of their tribes
    to teach their children well.

6 For generations yet to come
    must have them in their mind,
To tell their children how to keep
    and follow them in kind.

7 Then all will put their trust in God
    Who holds them in His hands;
So they will not forget to keep
    His precepts and commands.

8 They will not live like those of old
    who never would obey,
Whose spirits pulled away from God,
    and hearts were far away.

⁹ Nor will they be like Ephraim's men
   with bowstrings pulled to fight,
Who when they reached the battlefield
   turned round and took to flight.

¹⁰ Too many people in the past
   ignored God's covenant,
Refusing to obey His word
   and to His law assent.

¹¹ They failed to think about His works
   and wonders of His hand,
The miracles He'd shown to them
   and done throughout the land.

¹² For awesome were the mighty acts
   and marvels He had shown,
Within the land of Egypt's rule
   and on the fields of Zoan.

¹³ God sent a wind to split the sea
   and bade it to obey;
The churning waters stood apart
   to open up a way.

¹⁴ God led His people on a path
   by cloud when it was light;
He guided them when darkness fell
   by fire in the night.

¹⁵ God fractured rocks when all was parched
   by desert winds and heat;
Then water gushed up from the earth,
   a spring forever sweet.

¹⁶ God summoned forth a mighty stream
   from rocks that gave it birth,
A stream that like a river flows
   across and through the earth.

¹⁷ But still God's people disobeyed
    by breaking every law,
Rebelling in the wilderness
    with no regret at all.

¹⁸ They challenged God and tested Him
    according to their will,
Insisting that He give them food
    so they could eat their fill.

¹⁹ They spoke against His awesome might
    and power of His hand;
They questioned if He'd spread a feast
    within that barren land.

²⁰ Though God called water from a rock
    amid the desert heat,
Yet still they did not trust in Him
    to give them bread and meat.

²¹ And when God heard their words of doubt,
    His anger burned within;
He seethed at Israel's deceit
    and raged at Jacob's sin.

²² For they did not have faith in God
    or trust He'd make things right;
They did not think His hand would move
    to save them by its might.

²³ But yet God sought to rescue them
    and issued a command –
That heaven's doors be opened wide
    to pour upon the land.

²⁴ A rain of manna fell on them –
    the bounty of His bread,
The grain of heaven from His hand
    so everyone was fed.

⁴¹ The Holy One of Israel
    was angered and distressed,
Because of how they disobeyed
    and put Him to the test.

⁴² Not one of them remembered Him
    or that He struck the blows,
That rescued and redeemed their lives
    and saved them from their foes.

⁴³ They did not think about His works
    or wondrous signs He'd shown,
Within the land of Egypt's rule
    and on the fields of Zoan.

⁴⁴ For there God turned the streams to blood,
    which made the waters stink;
He fouled the rivers bank to bank
    till none was fit to drink.

⁴⁵ He sent a massive horde of pests,
    a swarming host of flies,
And hungry and destructive frogs
    that rained down from the skies.

⁴⁶ He blew in locusts on the wind
    that ate up crops of wheat,
And worms that chewed through fields of grain
    till naught was left to eat.

⁴⁷ He poured down ice and freezing rain,
    so thick that none could see,
Destroying everything that grows
    on spreading vine and tree.

⁴⁸ He struck the earth with lightning bolts
    like darts within a gale;
He pummeled cattle in the fields
    with waves of sleet and hail.

⁴⁹ He did not let His fury wane,
    nor did He stay His wrath,
But sent His angels to avenge
    and strike those in their path.

⁵⁰ He made a way that augured death
    and sounded forth a dirge;
He spared not one beyond the curse
    of darkest plague and scourge.

⁵¹ He killed each firstborn in the land –
    the heir and eldest son;
Egyptians from the root of Ham
    then knew that they were done.

⁵² It's then God led His people through
    the burning desert sand,
Just like a shepherd leads a flock
    with rod and staff in hand.

⁵³ He guided them so no one feared
    the tumult of the sea;
He kept them safe from crushing waves
    that drowned the enemy.

⁵⁴ And then He brought them to the hills
    within His holy land,
The mountains He had overwhelmed
    and gained by His right hand.

⁵⁵ God drove the nations far away,
    dividing what remained,
So Israel would have a home
    and live where He ordained.

⁵⁶ But still they tested God Most High,
    rebelling at His cause;
They did not follow His decrees
    or keep His holy laws.

⁵⁷ For like their ancestors of old,
    their hearts did not stay true,
Much like a bow that breaks its string
    when foes come into view.

⁵⁸ They angered and provoked the Lord
    with shrines they built on high;
He seethed when idols from their hands
    were lifted to the sky.

⁵⁹ When seeing their depravity,
    God let His wrath be known;
He spurned the tribes of Israel
    so they were on their own.

⁶⁰ He left His tabernacle courts
    and Shiloh where He dwelled,
Abandoning the tent He pitched
    because they had rebelled.

⁶¹ He sent the glory of His ark,
    the splendor of His hand,
Into the adversary's grasp
    within a foreign land.

⁶² He gave His people to the sword
    and let them be destroyed;
He raged at His inheritance
    for evil they enjoyed.

⁶³ The young men were consumed by flames
    because of all their wrongs;
The young maids did not celebrate
    or hear their wedding songs.

⁶⁴ The priests were thrown upon the ground
    and put to death by spears;
Their widows could not mourn for them,
    their eyes could shed no tears.

⁶⁵ But then the Lord awoke from sleep
    like one who's been reclined,
Or like a soldier sobering
    from wine that fogs the mind.

⁶⁶ He threw His adversaries down
    like rain beats back a flame;
He humbled foes and put their lives
    to everlasting shame.

⁶⁷ He spurned the tent of Joseph's seed
    because they were not true;
He turned from those of Ephraim's flesh,
    and did not see them through.

⁶⁸ But He bestowed on Judah's tribe
    the favor of His love;
And chose Mount Zion as His own,
    and set it high above.

⁶⁹ He built His sanctuary there,
    like heaven – high and pure;
He made it steady as the earth,
    which ever will endure.

⁷⁰ He called His servant David forth
    from where he tended sheep;
And took him from the herds he watched
    and guarded in his keep.

⁷¹ Yes, God brought David from his flocks
    to shepherd Israel,
To tend His people in the land
    where those of Jacob dwell.

⁷² And firmly David guided those
    whom God had set apart;
With skillful hands he tended them
    with pure and upright heart.

Psalm 79

¹ O God, Your foes have captured us,
　　Your land has been disgraced;
　Your temple courts have been defiled,
　　Jerusalem laid waste.

² They gave Your servants to the birds
　　to eat as carrion;
　They fed Your saints to savage beasts
　　as meat to chew upon.

³ They poured Your peoples' blood on streets
　　throughout Jerusalem;
　And there was no one who remained
　　whose hands could bury them.

⁴ The nations mock and laugh at us
　　as objects of their scorn;
　Their ridiculing leaves our souls
　　despondent and forlorn.

⁵ How long will You be angry, Lord?
　　How long will You be stern?
　How long will You prolong Your rage
　　and like a fire burn?

⁶ Lord, strike the nations in Your wrath,
　　their thoughts of You are few;
　They never call upon Your name
　　or put their trust in You.

⁷ For they've devoured Jacob's line,
　　the ones who are Your own;
　They've brought destruction to the land,
　　which once was Yours alone.

⁸ O do not strike us for the sins
　　our forbears did of old;
　But meet us with Your mercy, Lord,
　　for we must be consoled.

⁹ O God our Savior, help us now,
   for urgent are our needs;
And for the glory of Your name,
   forgive our sinful deeds.

¹⁰ The nations taunt us with their words,
   "Where is your God?" they say;
O Lord, declare how You'll avenge
   the blood they spill today.

¹¹ O hear the groans of those in chains
   and listen when they cry;
And by the power of Your arm,
   preserve those doomed to die.

¹² Repay the nations sevenfold
   for insults thrown at You;
Reproach them for their slander, Lord,
   and scornful words they spew.

¹³ Then we who are Your people, Lord,
   like sheep that safely graze,
Will give You thanks from age to age
   and ever sing Your praise.

Psalm 80

¹ O Shepherd Lord of Israel,
   Who guided Joseph's way,
May You who sit with cherubim
   receive our prayers today.

² For Ephraim and Manasseh's tribes
   and those of Benjamin,
Arise, O Lord, and show Your strength,
   deliver us from sin.

³ Restore us, God, and make us whole,
   redeem us by Your might;
And let Your face shine over us,
   forever in Your light.

⁴ How long, O God, Almighty One,
    how long will Your wrath blaze?
How long will You be angry, Lord,
    against the prayers we raise?

⁵ You feed us from a plate of grief
    to fill our hearts with woe;
You have us drink from massive bowls
    of tears that overflow.

⁶ You let our neighbors mock and jeer
    to make our shame complete,
And let our foes look down on us
    and laugh at our defeat.

⁷ Restore us, God, and make us whole,
    redeem us by Your might;
And let Your face shine over us
    forever in Your light.

⁸ From Egypt You removed a vine
    where it had long been bound;
You drove out nations in the way
    to plant it in the ground.

⁹ You cleared the hills and plowed the fields
    to place it with Your hand;
And when the vine was rooted deep,
    it grew to fill the land.

¹⁰ It overspread the mountain slopes
    it shaded with its leaves,
Its many branches covering
    the mighty cedar trees.

¹¹ It sent its branches far and wide,
    its progress never slowed;
It threw out shoots across the plains
    to where the river flowed.

12 So why, O God, have You allowed
a breach in every field?
And why have You let those who pass
eat freely from its yield?

13 For now this vine is food for boars
and every woodland beast,
And every creature on the ground
that hungers for a feast.

14 So turn again to us we plead,
Almighty God Divine;
Look down from heaven high above
to once more tend this vine.

15 O watch the root Your right hand placed
and nurtured as it grew,
The branch You strengthened for Yourself,
the one brought up by You.

16 For now the vine has been cut down
and burned among the weeds;
Rebuke the ones who did this, Lord,
and smite them for their deeds.

17 And let Your hand rest on the one
You raised up for Your own –
The son of man, Your chosen one,
who honors You alone.

18 Then we will never turn away
or let You be ignored;
Revive our lives, and we will call
upon Your name, O Lord.

19 Restore us, God, and make us whole,
redeem us by Your might;
And let Your face shine over us
forever in Your light.

Psalm 81

¹ O shout for joy to God, our strength,
    the One who makes us strong;
With voices raised to Jacob's God,
    let's sing a happy song.

² Strike up a tune and start to play
    the tambourine and flute;
And let the sweetest music rise
    from strings of harp and lute.

³ Blow trumpets when the moon is new
    and as the time draws near;
O sound the ram's horn on the day
    the full moon feast is here.

⁴ For Israel this is a rule,
    a statute and decree,
An ordinance from Jacob's God,
    His word for all to see.

⁵ God issued it for Joseph's house
    while crushing Egypt's might;
And then His people heard Him speak
    like thunder in the night.

⁶ *"I lifted loads that crushed your backs*
    so you would not be strained,
No longer would your hands be tied,
    no longer bound and chained.

⁷ *When trouble came I rescued you,*
    I answered from a cloud,
Then tested you at Meribah
    the way that I avowed.

⁸ *O people hear me when I speak*
    and listen to my word;
O Israel incline your ear
    so what I say is heard.

⁹ *You shall not worship other gods*
    or offer them a crown;
  You shall not have them in your midst
    nor even once bow down.

¹⁰ *For I am He, the Lord your God,*
    Who came to Egypt's land,
  To lead you out, and fill your mouths,
    and guide you with my hand.

¹¹ *But you, my people, would not turn*
    and listen to my plea;
  O Israel, you would not yield
    and bend your knee to me.

¹² *And so I let each stubborn will*
    become a heart of stone;
  I let you walk your chosen path
    to go your way alone.

¹³ *O how I wish you'd hear my words,*
    that you would listen well,
  That you would walk and ever be
    with me, O Israel.

¹⁴ *And if you would, then I would strike*
    and crush your enemy;
  I'd turn my hand against your foes,
    compelling them to flee.

¹⁵ *Then everyone who hates my name*
    would know their fate is sealed;
  They'd cringe to hear their punishment
    when finally revealed.

¹⁶ *But you, O Israel, would feast*
    on bread of finest wheat,
  And savor honey from the rock,
    forever pure and sweet."

Psalm 82

¹ God stands in heaven's court above
    from where He makes decrees;
He calls our judges to account
    for ruling as they please.

² God asks, *"How long will you defend*
    the wicked and unjust?
How long will you assist the vile
    and break your sacred trust?

³ *For you should help the destitute,*
    the homeless and distressed,
Defending those who need your aid –
    the helpless and oppressed.

⁴ *O save the weak and give them care*
    that comforts and consoles;
Deliver them from wicked hands
    that seek to crush their souls.

⁵ *O judges, don't you understand*
    your ways pervert what's right?
Your evil tears the world apart
    and turns the day to night.

⁶ *There was a time I thought of you*
    like gods born from above;
I made you children of my own
    because of my great love.

⁷ *But now like mortals you will die,*
    your life will pass away;
You'll fall like every other prince
    and end up in decay."

⁸ Arise, O God, it's time to judge
    those living in the lands,
Since all the nations everywhere
    are held within Your hands.

Psalm 83

1 O God, do not keep silent now,
   do not stay out of sight;
Do not be still or far away,
   and don't restrain Your might.

2 For those who hate Your name, O God,
   are starting to arise;
Your enemies are on the move
   and sending out their spies.

3 They plot with evil craftiness
   against those You hold close,
Conspiring against the ones
   whom You esteem the most.

4 Your foes are plotting to destroy
   the people You adore,
So that the name of Israel
   is spoken nevermore.

5 They hatch a plot against You, Lord,
   together they assent;
They join as one, and seal their plans
   upon a covenant.

6 The Hagrites join with many clans:
   the house of Ishmaelites,
The dynasty from Edom's land,
   and tribe of Moabites.

7 The Amaleks and Ammonites,
   the people of Gebal,
The Philistines and Tyre's hordes
   are gathered one and all.

8 And even the Assyrians
   have joined to take a spot,
To add their forces to the tribes
   descended down from Lot.

9 Lord, kill Your foes like Midian
and Sisera were slain,
Like Jabin died at Kishon brook –
in agony and pain.

10 Destroy Your enemies like those
who fell on Endor's plains,
Where scavengers picked over them
and scattered their remains.

11 Defeat their kings the way You struck
at Zebah and Oreb,
And how You tangled Zalmunna
and Zeeb within a web.

12 O treat Your enemies like those
who bragged they'd take the lands –
The lands that You possess, O God,
and hold within Your hands.

13 O make Your foes like dust that blows
through fields a drought has thinned;
And scatter them both far and wide
like chaff before the wind.

14 Engulf them like a heavy smoke
chokes all within its haze;
Consume them like a firestorm
that sets the hills ablaze.

15 Lord, overwhelm Your enemies
like bees within a swarm;
And terrify them as You ride
with wings upon the storm.

16 O bring them down and humble them,
defeated and in shame;
So all will see Your mighty hand
and call upon Your name.

¹⁷ Yes, let Your foes be mortified,
    with terror on their face;
And let them die in disrepute,
    dishonor and disgrace.

¹⁸ Lord, do these things that all may know
    the name of greatest worth,
That You alone are Lord Most High,
    supreme above the earth.

Psalm 84

¹ O Lord, how lovely is the place
    You dwell both day and night,
How beautiful Your temple shines,
    how wonderful its light.

² My soul yearns for Your temple courts,
    for there my spirit longs;
My heart and flesh cry out for You
    while bursting forth with songs.

³ For like a sparrow needs a nest
    with chicks beneath its wing,
So I must have Your altar near,
    O Lord, my God and King.

⁴ How happy those who know Your house
    and live there all their days;
For they will always worship You
    and ever sing Your praise.

⁵ And yes, how happy those whose strength
    is found in You alone;
Their hearts are set on Zion's hills
    to make Your glory known.

⁶ Through Baca Valley they must trek
    across its arid plains;
But yet for them it's filled with springs
    and blessed by autumn rains.

⁷ Their strength increases as they walk
    through many days and nights,
Until each one appears to You
    on Zion's lofty heights.

⁸ Lord God Almighty, hear my prayer,
    my heartfelt cry and plea;
O God of Jacob, listen now
    and turn Your ear to me.

⁹ O look upon our king and shield
    who glistens in the sun;
Yes, look with favor on the face
    of Your anointed one.

¹⁰ For one day in Your courts exceeds
    a thousand far away;
I'd rather stand outside Your gates
    than rest with those who stray.

¹¹ O Lord, You are our sun and shield,
    You bless us by Your grace;
You won't refuse whatever's good
    to those who seek Your face.

¹² O Lord of hosts, Almighty One,
    great God of heaven's might,
How happy those who trust in You
    and walk within Your light.

Psalm 85

¹ O Lord, You once were merciful
    and kindly to Your land,
Returning Jacob from afar
    by power of Your hand.

² You poured forgiveness like the rain
    on those who'd gone astray;
You covered their iniquities,
    and took their sins away.

3 You stayed the fury of Your might,
    Your anger that had blazed;
You doused the burning flames of wrath
    that passionately raged.

4 O God, our Savior, bring us back,
    restore us now to You;
O let Your indignation end,
    Your grievances be through.

5 O will Your present anger burn
    and ire not decrease?
And will Your wrath forever flame
    and fury never cease?

6 O strengthen and revive us, Lord,
    protect us as Your own;
So all Your people will again
    rejoice in You alone.

7 Come shower us with mercy, Lord,
    and Your unending love;
Draw near and meet us in our need,
    and save us from above.

8 O I have heard the Lord God pledge
    His peace for all our days;
But we, His saints, must not return
    to our imprudent ways.

9 For His salvation has come near
    to those who fear His name;
And there His glory will remain,
    forevermore the same.

10 Then faithfulness and love will walk
    in joyfulness and bliss;
And righteousness and peace will touch,
    embracing with a kiss.

¹¹ For faithfulness springs from the earth,
    arising like a dove;
While heaven pours down righteousness
    from stores of grace and love.

¹² The Lord provides the goods we need,
    the crops in every field;
He warms the land that grows the grain
    until we taste its yield.

¹³ For righteousness will lead the way,
    and truth will be restored;
And justice will prepare a path
    that goes before the Lord.

Psalm 86

¹ O Lord, please hear me when I cry
    and call out in distress;
For I am weak and destitute,
    there's nothing I possess.

² O Lord, my God, please guard my life,
    preserve and keep my soul;
I trust in You to care for me,
    to save and make me whole.

³ Be loving and kind-hearted, Lord,
    be merciful to me;
For all day long I lift my voice
    so You will hear my plea.

⁴ O fill my heart with happiness
    and joy for each new day;
For it's to You I lift up my soul
    as gratefully I pray.

⁵ For You, O Lord, are good and just,
    forgiving us anew;
You demonstrate Your awesome love
    to all who call on You.

⁶ So listen to my prayer, O Lord,
  and hear me when I cry;
I need Your mercy and Your grace
  so do not pass me by.

⁷ I'll call on You when trouble comes
  and I am in despair,
With confident and grateful heart
  that You will hear my prayer.

⁸ O there is not a god like You
  who's done what You have done;
There's no one who compares to You,
  there simply is not one.

⁹ One day the nations that You made
  will gather to rejoice,
To glorify and praise Your name,
  and worship with one voice.

¹⁰ For You are great and marvelous
  and do amazing things;
You stand alone as God Most High
  with glory on Your wings.

¹¹ So teach me how to follow You
  that truth will be my aim;
Unite my heart that it will seek
  to fear and love Your name.

¹² O Lord my God, I give You thanks
  and worship You with praise;
Forever will I lift Your name
  and glorify Your ways.

¹³ I know Your love for me is great
  for You alone can save;
You lifted me when I was lost
  and snatched me from the grave.

¹⁴ Yet I am overcome by thugs,
   the wicked and the vain,
A violent and a ruthless band
   that treats You with disdain.

¹⁵ But You, O Lord, are merciful,
   compassionate and fair;
You're slow to let Your anger show,
   with grace beyond compare.

¹⁶ Be gracious now and turn to me,
   renew my strength I pray;
O save me for my mother's sake
   who served You every day.

¹⁷ And demonstrate Your goodness, Lord,
   so all my foes can see;
Let them be shamed because Your hand
   protects and comforts me.

Psalm 87

¹ The city of the Lord is set
   upon His holy hill;
He's planted its foundation there
   according to His will.

² The Lord delights to see the gates
   created by His hand;
He loves them more than all the tents
   of Jacob in the land.

³ O Zion, you are glorious,
   how wonderful your name;
O city of the living God,
   the nations spread your fame.

⁴ For you are known by Babylon
   and Philistia too,
By Tyre, Cush, and Rahabites,
   who all acknowledge You.

⁵ O many will call Zion *"home,"*
   the city of their birth,
  The holy place the Lord Most High
   established on the earth.

⁶ The Lord will count each person born
   in Zion's lofty air;
  He'll mark them in His register
   of those residing there.

⁷ And they will make the sweetest sounds
   as joyfully they sing,
  "O Zion is a fount of joy –
  an ever-flowing spring."

Psalm 88

¹ Lord God of my salvation come
   and save me from my plight;
  I cry to You throughout the day
   and deep into the night.

² Please listen when I raise my voice
   and call to You in prayer;
  Incline Your ear to hear my woes
   and things I cannot bear.

³ My soul is bound with troubles, Lord,
   like shackles on a slave;
  My life is on the verge of death
   and drawing near the grave.

⁴ I feel like one about to die
   and fall into the pit,
  Like one whose strength has shriveled up,
   no longer strong or fit.

⁵ For I am treated like the dead
   who lie within the grave,
  Like one whom You do not recall
   or raise Your hand to save.

⁶ You dropped me in the lowest tomb
 where all is bare and stark,
The deepest trench, a gaping hole,
 a place forever dark.

⁷ Your wrath is unrelenting, Lord,
 there's nowhere I can flee;
It overwhelms me like the waves
 that crash upon the sea.

⁸ You've taken those who were my friends
 and made them into foes;
I turn but cannot get away,
 I'm overcome by woes.

⁹ My eyes are weak from suffering
 and crying in despair;
So every day I call to You
 and spread my hands in prayer.

¹⁰ O Lord, how can You show Your deeds
 to those who've died away?
How can departed people rise
 and praise Your name today?

¹¹ How can Your love and faithfulness
 be honored in the pit?
How can Your mercy be declared
 or witnessed from the crypt?

¹² How can the marvels You perform
 be known where there's no light?
How can the righteous acts You do
 be seen where there's no sight?

¹³ O Lord, a heartfelt cry for help
 remains my only prayer;
And this I offer up to You
 upon the morning air.

¹⁴ So why, O Lord, do You reject
   and turn away from me?
   Why do You never show Your face
   despite my anguished plea?

¹⁵ For I have suffered from my youth,
   I'm always close to death;
   I'm burdened by Your punishments
   that sap my life and breath.

¹⁶ Your anger and Your rage consume
   and overwhelm my soul;
   Your terrors have destroyed my life
   so I'm no longer whole.

¹⁷ And all day long Your wrath, O Lord,
   engulfs me like the tide;
   It rushes in surrounding me
   with swells on every side.

¹⁸ You've taken from me those I love
   and on whom I depend;
   Till darkness that engulfs my soul
   is now my only friend.

Psalm 89

¹ O Lord, I will forever sing
   about Your faithfulness;
   So every generation knows
   the love by which You bless.

² And I will tell how wonderful
   and steadfast is Your love,
   How faithful You have shown Yourself
   from heaven up above.

³ For You declared a covenant,
   a promise You revealed;
   You swore this word to David, Lord,
   a solemn pledge You sealed.

⁴ You told him that his lineage
    would sit upon his throne,
Throughout the ages yet to come,
    preserved by You alone.

⁵ O Lord, the heavens show Your works,
    exalting You with praise,
Attesting to Your faithfulness
    to those who keep Your ways.

⁶ For who in heaven equals You?
    Who is there to compare?
Is there a god who's like You, Lord?
    Is anyone so fair?

⁷ Within the council of the just,
    Your name is greatly feared;
Above all other powers, Lord,
    Your presence is revered.

⁸ Almighty God, O Lord of hosts,
    is anyone like You?
O there is none whose faithfulness
    will ever be as true.

⁹ You rule the waves that pound the shore,
    You calm the roaring seas;
You still the rising ocean gale
    and slow it to a breeze.

¹⁰ You crushed the evil powers, Lord,
    beneath the ocean waves;
You scattered all Your enemies
    and sent them to their graves.

¹¹ You shaped the heavens high above,
    You formed the skies and earth;
Yes, You created all the world
    and everything of worth.

12 You made the north and forged the south
    so songs of joy would rain;
  Mount Tabor and Mount Hermon sing
    when hearing of Your name.

13 There's might and power in Your arm,
    there's strength within Your hand;
  Your right hand has been lifted up
    for You are in command.

14 O righteousness and justice, Lord,
    are anchors of Your throne;
  While faithfulness and love are how
    Your kingdom will be known.

15 How happy those whose hearts rejoice
    and in You take delight,
  And those who put their trust in You
    and walk within Your light.

16 And all day long they praise Your name,
    together with one voice,
  And in Your righteousness find strength
    and thankfully rejoice.

17 For You give us the glory, Lord,
    by You our hands are strong;
  Through You we march triumphantly,
    in You the victor's song.

18 O Lord, You granted us a king
    to be a shining shield;
  O God of Israel, You planned
    the power he would wield.

19 For in a vision long ago,
    You said to those You love:
  *"I've given strength to one young man
    and helped him from above.*

²⁰ *I made my servant David king*
        and blessed him as my own;
    With oil I anointed him
        to sit upon the throne.

²¹ *My presence will be ever near*
        to keep him safe from harm;
    And I will surely strengthen him
        by power of my arm.

²² *No enemy will make a threat*
        or trick him with their lies;
    The wicked will not humble him
        so he cannot arise.

²³ *I'll press his adversaries down,*
        I'll crush his enemies;
    I'll strike his foes in front of him
        and bring them to their knees.

²⁴ *My faithfulness will not depart,*
        my love will never leave;
    And by the power of my name,
        great marvels he'll achieve.

²⁵ *For I will have him rule the seas*
        and keep them by his hand;
    And all will do what he decrees
        and follow his command.

²⁶ *He'll lift his voice and call to me,*
        'My Father and my Lord,
    You are my Savior and the Rock
        by Whom I am restored.'

²⁷ *I'll designate him as my heir,*
        the first one given birth;
    And he alone will reign supreme
        above the kings on earth.

28 *My love for him will never dim,*
   my care will not grow stale;
My covenant will never end,
   my pledge will never fail.

29 *And I will build his royal line*
   so ever they will reign;
His throne will last from age to age
   as long as skies remain.

30 *But if his heirs forsake my law,*
   and if they do not care,
Or if they do not keep my ways
   and think I'm not aware —

31 *Or if they stray from my commands,*
   rejecting my decrees,
Or if they don't abide with me
   but do the things they please —

32 *Then I will strike them with the rod*
   to punish every sin;
I'll make them suffer for their wrongs
   and feel my discipline.

33 *Yet I will not withhold my love*
   or keep it far away;
But I will show my faithfulness
   to David every day.

34 *I will not break my covenant*
   or go against my word;
For what I've spoken with my mouth
   will not be changed or blurred.

35 *For I have promised by my name*
   and sworn to carry through,
That what I pledged to David's ears
   is accurate and true.

³⁶ *His lineage will never end,*
   it will not be undone;
Forever will his crown remain,
   enduring like the sun.

³⁷ *His kingdom will be permanent*
   like moonlight in the sky –
An ever-present guardian,
   a witness set on high."

³⁸ But God, You now reject the king
   and treat him with disdain;
Your wrath and fury rages on,
   Your anger does not wane.

³⁹ For You have spurned Your covenant,
   abandoning Your trust;
You've let Your servant's crown be marred
   and sullied in the dust.

⁴⁰ You've broken down his city walls
   and left them to decay;
You've battered and You've pummeled him
   and filled him with dismay.

⁴¹ And all who pass have plundered him
   the way a sheep is shorn,
His neighbors showing their distain,
   rebuking by their scorn.

⁴² You turned him over to defeat,
   gave triumph to his foes;
You let his enemies rejoice
   and feast upon his woes.

⁴³ You dulled the edges of his blade,
   the temper of his sword;
And when the tide of battle turned,
   You looked away, O Lord.

44 You brought his glory to an end,
    no more will it be found;
You seized his kingdom and his throne
    and cast them to the ground.

45 You cut his youthful days too short
    like wind snuffs out a flame;
You piled him with indignities
    and covered him with shame.

46 How long will You be hidden Lord?
    How long till You return?
How long will You be filled with rage?
    How long will Your wrath burn?

47 Remember just how short our days,
    how fleeting is our life.
Have you created people, Lord,
    to know just grief and strife?

48 For who is there forever young,
    who lives and never dies?
Who keeps the hand of death away
    and meets not their demise?

49 O Lord, where is Your faithfulness?
    Where is Your ancient love?
And where are David's promises
    You swore down from above?

50 Do not forget Your servant, Lord,
    and how he's suffered scorn,
The way the wicked mock his name,
    and how his life is torn.

51 Remember how Your servant king
    is taunted and defamed,
How Your anointed one is mocked
    and constantly is shamed.

⁵² Yet I will praise and worship You,
    then praise You once again;
All glory be unto Your name,
    now Amen and Amen.

Psalm 90

¹ O Lord, You've always been our hope,
    a place where we can dwell,
Through generations without end,
    our home where all is well.

² Before You formed the earth and sky,
    the mountains and the sea,
You were eternally the Lord
    and evermore will be.

³ Yet we are but a moment, Lord,
    who soon will pass away;
Since dust we were and dust we'll be
    and will forever stay.

⁴ For in Your eyes a thousand years
    are like a day gone by,
A watch that passes in the dark
    more swiftly than a sigh.

⁵ You sweep us off as in a flood
    that rises in the night;
For we are fragile like the grass
    that sprouts at dawn's first light.

⁶ We start our day as tender plants
    that spring up with the dew,
But fade away by eventide
    when dry and withered through.

⁷ Our souls are shaken by Your wrath,
    our lives are torn and frayed;
And by the anger You pour out,
    our spirits are dismayed.

⁸ You know each sin that we commit,
    and our iniquity;
  You place them clearly in Your light
    where all of them You see.

⁹ Our days are passing rapidly
    because of wrath You've shown;
  Our years are quickly fading by
    and ending with a groan.

¹⁰ Just ten and sixty are our years,
    or eighty if we try;
  Yet they are filled with misery
    until the day we die.

¹¹ Who knows the power of Your wrath,
    the terror of Your might?
  And who has felt Your anger, Lord,
    and turned away in fright?

¹² O teach us how to count our days,
    to watch them from the start,
  To use our time so we may gain
    a wise and knowing heart.

¹³ How long, O Lord, will You be gone?
    How long till You return?
  Have pity on Your servants, Lord,
    and show us Your concern.

¹⁴ Each morning fill our souls, O Lord,
    with love that will endure,
  So we may sing a joyful song
    that cheers us evermore.

¹⁵ Remember our afflictions, Lord,
    the years consumed by woe;
  Return as many days of joy,
    and let our gladness show.

16 And may the wonder of Your deeds
forever be retold;
So they'll be known by those You love,
Your servants young and old.

17 O let Your love and kindness, Lord,
affirm us in our plans;
And bless the service of the work
accomplished by our hands.

Psalm 91

1 Whoever dwells with God Most High
is kept from many harms;
For those who seek to be with Him
are safe within His arms.

2 My lips will say these words to Him,
"O Lord, You are my rest,
A fortress where I put my trust,
a refuge where I'm blessed."

3 For surely God will watch your steps
from tripping in the snare,
And keep you safe from all disease
so you will not despair.

4 Just like a bird protects its young
beneath its outstretched wing,
God's faithfulness will be your shield,
a rock on which to cling.

5 And you will never know the grip
of terror in the night,
Or any arrow flying high
upon the morning light.

6 Nor will there be a pestilence
to dread when day is gone,
Or any epidemic scourge
to fear when comes the dawn.

⁷ A thousand may fall in your path,
    ten thousand at your side;
  Yet you will not be touched or harmed,
    no evil will betide.

⁸ Your eyes will look upon the vile
    and others who have sinned;
  And you will see their punishment
    and how they're disciplined.

⁹ So always make the Most High God
    your refuge and your home;
  Continue holding to the Lord,
    and from Him never roam.

¹⁰ Then no disaster will approach,
    no threat will cause dismay;
  No plague will enter where you dwell
    or harm you on your way.

¹¹ For God will have His angels hold
    and keep you in their gaze,
  To follow closely where you go
    and guard you all your days.

¹² They'll lift and hold you in their hands
    when danger is around;
  So you won't stumble on a stone
    and fall upon the ground.

¹³ And you will kick the lion's head
    and tread upon the snake;
  The strongest lion you will crush,
    the cobra you will break.

¹⁴ *"Because you love me,"* says the Lord,
    "I'll guard you carefully;
  Yes, I will watch and rescue you
    because you trust in me.

¹⁵ *So when you're down and in distress*
and call upon my name,
I'll answer and deliver you
and take away your shame.

¹⁶ *And I will give you many years*
to be your just reward;
And you will know, and taste, and see
salvation from the Lord."

Psalm 92

¹ O Lord, how good to honor You
with joyful songs of praise;
O God Most High, I'll worship You
for now and all my days.

² I love to sing about Your love
upon the morning light,
And tell of Your great faithfulness
when darkness fills the night.

³ I love to please You as I play
the lyre and the flute,
And offer You a melody
from strings of harp and lute.

⁴ For I delight in what You've done,
Your deeds throughout the lands;
I sing for joy at every work
created by Your hands.

⁵ O Lord, how mighty are Your acts,
how greatly they astound;
And how amazing are Your thoughts,
how deep and how profound.

⁶ Yet fools will never understand
the things that You decree;
For there is much they do not know
and one thing they can't see –

⁷ That while the wicked seem to thrive
 like grass that grows with rain,
They will be crushed and beaten down
 and never seen again.

⁸ O Lord, Your reign is from on high,
 exalted over all;
Forever You will be supreme
 and never yield or fall.

⁹ For surely all Your enemies,
 the vile and those who sin,
Will shrivel like the autumn leaves
 when scattered to the wind.

¹⁰ But You have made me stronger than
 an ox that roams the land;
With oil You've anointed me –
 a blessing from Your hand.

¹¹ My eyes have looked upon my foes
 and witnessed their demise;
I've seen them conquered and destroyed
 and heard their anguished cries.

¹² The righteous, though, will ever thrive
 like palm trees in the sun;
They'll grow up tall like cedar trees
 that rise in Lebanon.

¹³ For they are planted in the house,
 the temple of the Lord;
And flourishing within His courts
 will be their just reward.

¹⁴ Their lives will ever bear much fruit
 though growing old and grey;
Their hearts will be forever young
 with strength for each new day.

15 And they will sing, *"The Lord is just,*
     the King of Righteousness;
   There's nothing bad that dwells in Him,
     our Rock and One we bless."

Psalm 93

1 O Lord, You're robed in majesty
     and govern by Your hand;
   The world established by Your strength
     will surely ever stand.

2 Your throne is from long ages past,
     Your kingdom's born of old;
   O You are everlasting, Lord,
     from timelessness untold.

3 O Lord, the oceans rise and fall,
     the waves come crashing in;
   The seas are like a shouting voice
     that's heard above the din.

4 But You indeed are mightier
     than any ocean squall;
   With strength that crushes surf and tide,
     You rule above them all.

5 O Lord, Your laws stand strong and firm,
     Your word is true and pure;
   Your temple is a holy place
     and will be evermore.

Psalm 94

1 O Lord, avenge us from the vile,
     O be a choking vine;
   Shine forth, O God, retaliate,
     and let Your justice shine.

² Arise, O Lord, and take a stand,
    to judge the earth anew;
And give the proud what they deserve,
    repay them what they're due.

³ How long, O Lord, will evil reign?
    How long will it prevail?
How long until the wicked fall?
    How long until they fail?

⁴ The wicked spew forth vicious words
    with arrogance and pride;
Their boasting tongues reveal their crimes
    and sin that dwells inside.

⁵ The wicked crush Your people, Lord,
    and grind them in the dust,
Oppressing Your inheritance
    in ways that are unjust.

⁶ The wicked slay the alien
    and widow in distress;
They murder those who are alone
    and kill the fatherless.

⁷ The wicked think You do not see,
    they say, *"The Lord is blind;*
The God of Jacob pays no heed,
    He gives our deeds no mind."

⁸ Take care, you fools, you senseless ones,
    and open up your eyes.
How long will you be ignorant
    and ever so unwise?

⁹ For does the Lord who gave you ears
    not hear the things you say?
And does the One who gave you eyes
    not see you when you stray?

¹⁰ And does the Lord who disciplines
    not punish prince and king?
O does the One who teaches all
    not fathom everything?

¹¹ The Lord knows each and every thought
    that dwells within the brain;
He knows that they are fleeting breaths,
    mere folly and in vain.

¹² O Lord, how happy are the ones
    whom You instruct with care;
How fortunate the ones You teach
    from laws that You declare.

¹³ You keep us safe from misery
    and trouble every day;
You slay the wicked for their ways
    and cast them far away.

¹⁴ O You will not repudiate
    the ones who are Your own;
You won't forsake Your people, Lord,
    or leave them all alone.

¹⁵ For judgment will again be fair
    with justice in the court;
The pure in heart will follow it
    and give it their support.

¹⁶ O who will rise in my defense
    when tongues are spitting bile?
And who will take a stand for me
    against the mean and vile?

¹⁷ O Lord, unless You care for me
    like one who helps a friend,
Then surely I will be dispatched
    and quickly meet my end.

¹⁸ For when my foot is slipping, Lord,
    You lift me by Your love;
You catch me when I trip and fall,
    You hold me from above.

¹⁹ And when the worries of the world
    begin to take their toll,
Your consolations lift me up,
    and joy engulfs my soul.

²⁰ But Lord, You won't abide with those
    who rule the way they please;
Nor will You tolerate a judge
    who issues bad decrees.

²¹ The wicked bind themselves as one
    and plot against the just,
Condemning them without a plea,
    returning them to dust.

²² O Lord, you are my strength and shield,
    You hold me with Your arm;
O God, You are a solid rock
    Who shelters me from harm.

²³ O surely You will strike the vile
    to punish every sin,
Destroying them for wrongful acts
    and evil thoughts within.

Psalm 95

¹ Come let us raise our voices high
    and sing unto the Lord;
Let's shout aloud to God our Rock
    and sound a joyous chord.

² O with thanksgiving, let us come
    and praise Him from our heart,
Extolling Him with harp and song
    to set His name apart.

³ The Lord is strong and powerful
    with glory in His wings,
A God above all other gods
    and mightier than kings.

⁴ For in His hand He holds the depths
    that undergird the earth,
The highest peaks and mountain tops
    and everything of worth.

⁵ God made the oceans and the seas,
    He formed them by His hand,
Then gathered them into one place
    to fashion solid land.

⁶ So come now let us worship God,
    the One who wears the crown;
To God our Maker let us kneel,
    in reverence bow down.

⁷ For He's our God, and we are His,
    the shepherd and His sheep;
He watches and He cares for us
    and holds us in His keep.

⁸ So listen now to what God says,
    "Don't turn your hearts away,
Or trip like those in Massah's wilds
    and Meribah that day.

⁹ *For there your parents tested me,*
    rebelling everyone,
Despite observing all my works
    and many things I'd done.

¹⁰ *My anger burned for forty years*
    for how they disobeyed,
A generation wandering
    because their hearts had strayed.

¹¹ *And so I swore a solemn oath*
that they would fail their quest –
To never reach their journey's end
and never know my rest."

Psalm 96

¹ O sing unto the Lord a song,
a new song let us sing;
Let all the earth join in this song
and let His praises ring.

² O sing unto the Lord a song,
a song that gives Him praise;
So His salvation is proclaimed
today and all our days.

³ Tell nations He is glorious,
magnificent and grand;
Proclaim the wonders of His acts
to people in the land.

⁴ For great and worthy is the Lord,
the One that we adore,
The One to fear above all gods,
the One to honor more.

⁵ While gods that other nations serve
are idols made of clay;
The Lord set out the firmament
and put it on display.

⁶ For majesty and splendor shine
from God who is our light;
While strength and beauty fill His courts
and show His awesome might.

⁷ So come now praise the Lord on high,
exalt Him in the lands;
O praise His glory and His strength
and power of His hands.

⁸ Yes, praise the splendor of the Lord,
    the glory of His name;
Bring offerings into His courts
    with joyful hearts aflame.

⁹ Give honor to God's majesty,
    His holiness and worth;
Submit and bow before the Lord,
    you nations of the earth.

¹⁰ Proclaim the news, *"The Lord God reigns,*
    He set the earth in place;
And He will come to judge the world
    with righteousness and grace."

¹¹ So let the heavens sing for joy,
    let all the earth rejoice;
Let every sea and ocean roar
    and creature raise its voice.

¹² Let every field be jubilant,
    and all that lives within;
Let all the forest trees rejoice,
    O let their song begin.

¹³ And they will sing before the Lord
    Who comes in righteousness,
To judge the earth in truth and love
    and through His faithfulness.

Psalm 97

¹ The Lord God reigns, He rules the world,
    all nature hears His voice;
So let the lands and seas be glad,
    let all the earth rejoice.

² Thick clouds and darkness circle Him
    and billow all around;
While righteousness and justice shine
    as anchors of His crown.

³ A fire goes before the Lord
  and burns so none can hide,
Consuming enemies in front
  and foes on every side.

⁴ His lightning bolts are shattering,
  they fill the world with light,
Illuminating all the earth,
  which trembles at His might.

⁵ Before the presence of the Lord,
  the mountains melt like wax;
Before the Lord of all the earth,
  they tumble when He acts.

⁶ The heavens show His righteousness,
  the skies declare His fame;
So all will know His majesty
  and glory of His name.

⁷ And those who worship images
  will reap their just reward,
By being shamed to see their gods
  bow down before the Lord.

⁸ O Lord, all Zion celebrates
  and Judah shouts with glee,
When hearing of the righteous laws
  and judgments You decree.

⁹ For You, O Lord, are God Most High
  Who reigns above the earth,
Exalted over other gods
  and everything of worth.

¹⁰ Let all who love the Lord respond
  by hating evil plans;
For God delivers those of faith
  from vile and wicked hands.

11 The Lord will brightly shine His light
    on those He sets apart;
So purest joy and happiness
    uplift the pure in heart.

12 Rejoice, you faithful, in the Lord,
    and give Him your acclaim;
Rejoice, you righteous, everywhere,
    and praise His holy name.

Psalm 98

1 O sing a new song to the Lord
    for marvels He has done;
By His right hand and holy arm
    the victory is won.

2 The Lord makes His salvation known,
    the power of His might;
He's shown His righteousness to all
    the nations in His sight.

3 The Lord recalls His faithfulness
    and love to Israel;
And God's salvation has been seen
    wherever people dwell.

4 So all the earth, now sing for joy,
    from mountains to the sea;
Burst forth with praises to the Lord,
    and sing the victory.

5 Make music to the Lord with harp,
    and play the sweetest sound;
Rejoice with songs that praise the Lord
    so harmonies resound.

6 With trumpets and the sound of horns,
    lift up your voice and sing;
Sing joyful praises to the Lord,
    and shout to God, our King.

[7] And let the seas and oceans roar
 and all that they contain;
 Let all the world reverberate,
 let no one be restrained.

[8] Let streams and rivers clap their hands,
 in rhythm harmonize;
 And let the mountains sing for joy
 and echo in reprise.

[9] Yes, let them sing before the Lord,
 the One of endless worth;
 For He will judge in righteousness
 the people of the earth.

Psalm 99

[1] The Lord God reigns above the earth,
 let people shake and groan;
 He sits between the cherubim
 ensconced upon His throne.

[2] The Lord of Zion is renowned
 and grander than all things,
 Above the nations of the earth,
 supreme above their kings.

[3] Let all the people praise You, Lord,
 with joyful tongues proclaim,
 That You are great and wonderful
 and awesome is Your name.

[4] For justice, strength, and righteousness,
 You love, O King of might;
 To Jacob You've shown equity
 and done what's good and right.

[5] So let's exalt the Lord our God
 with praises that are sweet;
 Because He is the Holy One,
 let's worship at His feet.

⁶ Like Moses, let us trust in God,
    like Aaron, call His name;
Like Samuel, reach out to Him,
    and He'll respond the same.

⁷ For from the pillar of the cloud,
    He called them with His word;
And they adhered to His decrees
    and statutes that they heard.

⁸ O Lord our God, You answered them,
    forgiving Israel;
And though You punished all their sins,
    You guarded them as well.

⁹ So come exalt the Lord our God,
    and praise with one accord;
O worship at His sacred hill
    for holy is the Lord.

Psalm 100

¹ O shout for joy unto the Lord,
    and praise Him with your voice;
O come now people of the earth
    be grateful and rejoice.

² O worship Him with happy hearts
    that yearn for just one thing –
To come before the Lord with songs
    that joyfully you sing.

³ O know that He, the Lord is God
    Who made us by His hand;
For we're His people that He tends,
    the sheep upon His land.

⁴ O let thanksgiving fill His gates
    and drown His courts with praise;
Give blessings to His holy name,
    and thank Him for His ways.

⁵ The Lord is good and merciful,
    His love will long endure;
  His faithfulness and truth sustains
    His people evermore.

Psalm 101

¹ O Lord, I will forever praise
    the wonder of Your love,
  And sing about Your righteousness
    and justice from above.

² I long to live a blameless life –
    O won't You come to me?
  Within my house I'll keep my heart
    in upright purity.

³ No wrongful deeds will I behold,
    or set before my eyes;
  The actions faithless people take
    are something I despise.

⁴ The wicked will not gather near,
    the vile I'll not befriend;
  No evil will I tolerate,
    no hateful act defend.

⁵ My hands will silence slanderers
    for how they've schemed and lied;
  I'll not abide the arrogant
    or tolerate their pride.

⁶ My eyes will look for faithful souls
    who keep their honor pure;
  And they will serve me where I live
    and dwell with me secure.

⁷ But those who act deceitfully
    or lie to get their way,
  Will never dwell within my house
    or in my presence stay.

⁸ Each day I'll strike the wicked down,
    with death their just reward;
And they will not again approach
    the city of the Lord.

Psalm 102

¹ O Lord, please listen to my prayer
    and do not pass me by;
O see my pain and suffering,
    and hear my anguished cry.

² O don't conceal Your face from me
    when I'm about to fall;
But turn your ear and answer me,
    come quickly when I call.

³ My days are like mere puffs of smoke
    that vanish in a flash;
My bones are scorched as in a flame
    that burns a log to ash.

⁴ My heart has lost its energy,
    it withers like the grass;
My appetite's deserted me
    as days fly quickly past.

⁵ My grief exhausts and wearies me,
    I'm worn out from my groans;
My body is consumed by pain,
    my skin clings to my bones.

⁶ My life is like a pelican
    alone and far from sea,
Or like an owl that finds no rest
    or shelter in a tree.

⁷ I lie awake from dusk to dawn
    while thinking of my plight;
I'm like a bird upon a roof,
    deserted in the night.

⁸ My days are marked by enemies
    who shout at me or worse;
Their mockery and scornful words
    have made my name a curse.

⁹ My food is but a gritty mix
    of cinders, ash and clay;
My drink is mingled with my tears
    from weeping through the day.

¹⁰ You've shown Your wrath and anger, Lord,
    I've no place left to hide;
My life is taken from my hands,
    picked up and cast aside.

¹¹ My days are like a shadow's edge
    that fades when evening falls;
I shrivel like the summer grass
    that dies when winter calls.

¹² But You, O Lord, sit high above,
    ensconced upon Your throne;
From age to age You will endure,
    Your glory always known.

¹³ Arise, O Lord, let Zion feel
    Your merciful embrace;
For now is the appointed time
    to show her care and grace.

¹⁴ For all Your servants dearly love
    each one of Zion's stones;
And even thinking of its dust
    elicits heartfelt groans.

¹⁵ The nations soon will fear the Lord
    and tremble at His name;
The kings who walk the earth will know
    His glory and His fame.

¹⁶ The Lord will look on Zion's walls,
    rebuilding them anew;
Arrayed in glory He'll appear
    like sun upon the dew.

¹⁷ And He will hear the destitute
    who cry out in despair;
He won't despise a single plea
    or turn from any prayer.

¹⁸ So generations not yet born
    may give the Lord their praise,
O let these words be written down
    to tell about His ways:

¹⁹ *"The Lord once looked upon the land*
    from where He reigned on high;
From heaven He observed the earth
    by watching with His eye.

²⁰ *From there He looked on prisoners*
    and heard them cry and plea;
He pardoned those condemned to die
    and set the captives free."

²¹ And so within Jerusalem
    He'll see His banner raised;
In Zion He'll be lifted up
    and hear His name be praised.

²² For when the nations gather round
    and join with one accord,
They'll sing in joyful worshipping
    the praises of the Lord.

²³ And yet the Lord has weakened me
    and filled my eyes with tears;
His hand's rebuked me in my prime,
    foreshortening my years.

²⁴ O God, don't take my life away
    like one who is condemned;
Don't let me die before my time
    while Your days never end.

²⁵ For long ago You made the seas
    and measured out the earth;
Your hands designed the heavens, Lord,
    and everything of worth.

²⁶ And though Your works will be destroyed,
    You always will remain;
For You'll discard them like a shirt
    that's soiled with a stain.

²⁷ O surely You will never change,
    on that we can depend;
Forever You will stay the same,
    Your years will never end.

²⁸ O may our children live with You
    as those whom You adore;
And may Your servants and their heirs
    be with You evermore.

Psalm 103

¹ O praise and bless the Lord, my soul,
    with honor and acclaim;
Let every breath within me praise
    and bless His holy name.

² O praise and bless the Lord, my soul,
    for awesome are His gifts;
O praise the Lord and don't forget
    His many benefits.

³ The Lord forgives you for your sins
    and your iniquities;
The Lord heals every malady
    and cures you from disease.

⁴ The Lord redeems you from the pit
     and lifts you high above;
  He holds you in His tender care
     and crowns you with His love.

⁵ The Lord provides and fills your life
     with good and matchless things;
  He gives you strength so you can rise
     and soar on eagles' wings.

⁶ The Lord reveals His righteousness
     to those who are repressed;
  He works His justice for the poor,
     the outcasts, and oppressed.

⁷ The Lord told Moses of His ways
     and let His plans be known;
  He showed His deeds to Israel –
     to those who were His own.

⁸ The Lord is merciful and good,
     with caring from above;
  The Lord is slow to show His wrath
     and quick to prove His love.

⁹ The Lord won't always reprimand
     or chide us for our past;
  His rage will not forever burn,
     nor will His anger last.

¹⁰ The Lord won't mete out punishment
     for what our sin deserves,
  Nor pay us back for every wrong
     and evil He observes.

¹¹ For higher than the heavens are
     above the earth below,
  Much greater is the love He shows
     to those who fear Him so.

¹² As far as east is from the west,
    beyond the distant seas,
So far has He moved us away
    from our iniquities.

¹³ As parents show their children love
    without a word of shame,
The Lord shows care and gentleness
    to those who fear His name.

¹⁴ He knows that we were formed by Him
    and understands our worth;
He knows that we are simply specks
    of dust upon the earth.

¹⁵ For we are like the blades of grass
    and flowers in a field;
We flourish in the springtime rains
    when blooms are first revealed.

¹⁶ But soon the winds of autumn blow,
    the flowers fade away;
And no one sees them anymore
    for all lies still and grey.

¹⁷ And yet for those who fear the Lord,
    His love will never end;
And on their children's children will
    His righteousness descend.

¹⁸ The Lord stays close to those who hold
    and keep His covenant,
And all who faithfully obey
    His law and its intent.

¹⁹ The Lord set heaven high above,
    and there He placed His throne;
His kingdom now reigns over all
    the hidden and the known.

²⁰ So praise the Lord, angelic ones,
    arise and now be stirred;
  O praise the Lord, you mighty host
    and keepers of His word.

²¹ And praise the Lord, you holy ones,
    be thankful and rejoice;
  O praise Him, you who do His will,
    and listen to His voice.

²² O praise the Lord, all living things,
    His wondrous ways extol;
  In all of His dominion praise
    and bless Him, O my soul.

Psalm 104

¹ O Lord, my God, how great You are,
    my soul exalts Your name;
  For You are clothed in majesty,
    magnificence and fame.

² You draped Yourself as with a cloak,
    a covering of light;
  You stretched the heavens like a tent
    against the starry night.

³ You placed Your chambers in the skies,
    above all earthly things;
  You formed the clouds like chariots
    so wind would be their wings.

⁴ You made the winds Your messengers
    to do as You command,
  And soaring flames Your ministers
    while burning through the land.

⁵ You built a firm foundation, Lord,
    on which You set the earth,
  So strong that it cannot be moved
    though rocked for all its worth.

⁶ You hid the mountains underneath
    the waters of the deep,
  Which covered like a garment draped
    on one about to sleep.

⁷ At Your rebuke the waters fled
    and rushed away in fright;
  When thunder sounded from Your voice,
    they quickly took to flight.

⁸ You prearranged a place for them
    as from the hills they flowed;
  They rushed to valleys far below
    till land and mountains showed.

⁹ And thus You made the waters sink
    and stand beneath the shore –
  A line the waves can never cross
    to drown the earth once more.

¹⁰ O Lord, You make the bounding springs
    whose waters ever flow,
  Between the mountains and the hills
    to valleys far below.

¹¹ The waters quench the thirst of mules
    and beasts within the field;
  While animals on riverbanks
    drink freely from their yield.

¹² The birds are safe in trees that thrive
    where rivers rush along;
  They nest among the verdant leaves
    and sing a happy song.

¹³ O Lord, You drench the hills with rain,
    You water all the lands;
  The earth is nourished by the fruit
    created by Your hands.

¹⁴ You make the grass grow green and lush
    for cows and bulls to eat;
  You give us plants that we can tend
    and crops of grain and wheat.

¹⁵ You give us wine to cheer our hearts
    and oil for our face;
  You give us bread to keep us strong,
    You fill us by Your grace.

¹⁶ You plant the trees in Lebanon,
    great cedars on each hill;
  You water them abundantly
    so they can drink their fill.

¹⁷ Their branches are a habitat
    where birds can build their nest;
  The pine trees are a home for storks
    where they can find their rest.

¹⁸ The mountains are a spot where goats
    can live and safely graze;
  A place where badgers make their home,
    secure for all their days.

¹⁹ You make the moon to mark the months
    and seasons of the year,
  The sun to know the time to set
    and daily disappear.

²⁰ You make the dark a covering
    as day gives way to night;
  So forest beasts can prowl about
    while staying out of sight.

²¹ The lion roars ferociously
    while seeking out its prey;
  It looks for Your provision, Lord,
    to fill it every day.

²² And when the sun first shines its light
    on forest, field and fen,
The lion once again returns
    to rest within its den.

²³ Then people rise to face the day
    and do the work at hand;
They labor until eventide
    when light departs the land.

²⁴ O Lord, how wisely You have made
    so many splendid things;
The earth abounds with animals
    that move by legs and wings.

²⁵ The ocean creatures ply the deep
    and live by gill and claw,
So plentiful these living things,
    the mighty and the small.

²⁶ The sea is plowed by sailing ships
    and great Leviathan,
Which You created just for sport
    according to Your plan.

²⁷ And every being on the earth
    depends and waits on You;
For You provide their sustenance
    whenever it is due.

²⁸ You give them food to gather up
    so they are well supplied;
You hand it out abundantly
    till they are satisfied.

²⁹ But when You hide Your face from them,
    they tremble out of fear;
And when You take away their breath,
    to dust they disappear.

³⁰ For when You send Your Spirit, Lord,
    creating life anew,
They rise and see the earth and skies
    and all that comes from You.

³¹ O may the glory of the Lord
    endure forevermore;
And may He revel in His works
    that are from days of yore.

³² One look from God and all the earth
    is shaken by His glare;
One touch and mountains start to burn
    and smoke fills up the air.

³³ O I will sing unto the Lord
    as long as I have breath;
I'll sing the praises of my God
    till I'm consumed by death.

³⁴ So may my meditations rise
    and fill Him with delight;
And I will hope upon the Lord,
    rejoicing day and night.

³⁵ But may the wicked disappear
    and never be restored.
O bless and praise the Lord, my soul,
    O praise Him, praise the Lord.

Psalm 105

¹ Give thanks and praises to the Lord
    and call upon His name;
Tell all the nations of His deeds,
    His greatness and His fame.

² O let your voices sing to Him,
    rejoicing in His ways;
Proclaim the wonders He's performed
    with songs that give Him praise.

³ Give glory to His holy name
   and let Him be adored;
 Let joy and gladness fill the hearts
   of those who seek the Lord.

⁴ O look upon His awesome strength
   and power of His grace;
 And always go to Him for help,
   forever seek His face.

⁵ Remember all the deeds He's done,
   the things for which He's famed;
 And revel in His miracles
   and judgments He's proclaimed.

⁶ O listen heirs of Abraham
   and those of Jacob's seed,
 Yes, you the chosen of the Lord
   recall His every deed.

⁷ For He is Lord, our only God,
   the One of greatest worth;
 His justice is for all the world –
   for everyone on earth.

⁸ The Lord will keep His promises,
   the word of His command;
 A thousand generations hence
   His covenant will stand.

⁹ The Lord will honor what He swore
   to Isaac and His seed,
 His covenant with Abraham,
   the word He guaranteed.

¹⁰ The Lord confirmed His promises
   to Jacob by decree;
 And Israel received His pledge
   to last eternally.

¹¹ The Lord declared, *"I give the land*
of Canaan for your own –
A land as your inheritance,
to be for you alone."

¹² He made this pledge when they were weak,
in numbers they were few,
A band of nomads in the land,
mere strangers passing through.

¹³ They wandered through the wilderness
to nations far and wide,
Traversing kingdoms as they moved
with no place to abide.

¹⁴ The Lord let no one strike at them
or do them any harm;
He cautioned kings and overlords
to cause them no alarm.

¹⁵ The Lord declared, *"Don't touch the saints*
anointed in my name;
Don't hurt the prophets I appoint
or make them suffer pain."

¹⁶ The Lord spread famine through the land
till naught was left to eat;
He took away the staff of life,
the bread of grain and wheat.

¹⁷ But yet the Lord had made a way
through one who'd gone before,
By sending Joseph as a slave
to make their way secure.

¹⁸ Cold fetters shackled Joseph's feet,
preventing him from flight;
An iron collar choked his neck,
oppression was his plight.

¹⁹ He suffered thus, until his dreams
　　and visions came to pass;
　The prophecy that came from God
　　was proven true at last.

²⁰ The Pharaoh called for his release
　　and issued a decree –
　A royal order by his hand
　　for setting Joseph free.

²¹ Then Joseph ran the Pharaoh's lands
　　and all that he possessed –
　The Pharaoh's house and government,
　　for Joseph governed best.

²² And Joseph had authority
　　to judge both prince and lord,
　To teach the elders to be wise,
　　to punish and reward.

²³ Then Israel came down to dwell
　　and live as Egypt's guest;
　Yes, Jacob settled in that land
　　and found a place to rest.

²⁴ The Lord ensured their fruitfulness,
　　much like a vine that grows,
　Till they became more numerous
　　than those who were their foes.

²⁵ The Lord turned Egypt's hearts to stone
　　with hatred deep inside;
　Their rage against God's chosen ones
　　would not be mollified.

²⁶ And so the Lord sent Moses down
　　to those who were His own;
　And Aaron went along with him
　　so they'd not serve alone.

²⁷ In Egypt they worked miracles
   and wonders from the Lord,
Performing signs and mighty acts
   that could not be ignored.

²⁸ The Lord sent darkness to the land
   and everything was black;
For Egypt had not heeded Him
   but rather turned its back.

²⁹ The Lord changed rivers into blood
   that made the waters red,
Infecting all the life within
   till all the fish were dead.

³⁰ The Lord allowed a plague of frogs
   to cover everything;
They crawled into the palaces
   and bedroom of the king.

³¹ The Lord spoke out and there appeared
   a swarm of gnats and flies;
They flew through town and countryside
   and swept across the skies.

³² The Lord turned mist and gentle rain
   into a storm of hail,
With flashing bolts of lightning strikes
   like fire in a gale.

³³ The Lord stripped every living plant –
   the fig tree and the vine,
Destroying them so there would be
   no harvest fruit or wine.

³⁴ The Lord called locusts down on them
   in one gigantic swarm;
Grasshoppers that no one could count
   came crashing like a storm.

³⁵ The hordes ate everything that grew –
    the petals and the shoots,
The produce from the tended fields,
    the flowers to the roots.

³⁶ The Lord then struck the final blow –
    the firstborn in the land;
The first fruits of their legacy
    were smitten by His hand.

³⁷ The Lord delivered Israel
    from out of Egypt's hold;
He led them forth with precious goods
    of silver and of gold.

³⁸ And Egypt filled with dread and fear,
    and staggered by the blow,
Saw Israel depart their land
    and gladly let them go.

³⁹ The Lord spread out a cloud by day
    and fire by the night;
The one to give a covering,
    the other as a light.

⁴⁰ They asked, and He provided quail
    to be their source of meat;
He gave them manna from above
    as heaven's bread to eat.

⁴¹ The Lord brought water from a rock
    that opened with His blow;
It bubbled up through desert sands,
    and like a river flowed.

⁴² The Lord recalled His Holy word,
    the covenant He made,
His promise made to Abraham,
    the hope that He conveyed.

⁴³ And so He led His people out
    as they rejoiced in song,
The chosen ones, the set apart,
    a happy shouting throng.

⁴⁴ The Lord took lands the nations held
    and gave them to His own;
So they would reap the benefit
    that other hands had sown.

⁴⁵ The Lord did this so they might keep
    His precepts and His law;
So praise the Lord for what He's done,
    O praise Him one and all.

Psalm 106

¹ O praise the Lord for He is good,
    His love will long endure;
Give thanks to Him and bless His name
    both now and evermore.

² Can anyone proclaim His deeds
    and wonders of His ways?
Can any thank the Lord enough
    and shower Him with praise?

³ His blessings come to those who act
    with justice in His sight,
And those who seek to keep His law
    by doing what is right.

⁴ O Lord, do not forsake me now,
    and do not turn away;
But when You save Your people, Lord,
    please rescue me, I pray.

⁵ And when You bless Your chosen ones
    then I will lift my voice,
And join with Your inheritance
    to praise You and rejoice.

⁶ O like our ancestors we've sinned
        and turned from just decrees;
    For evil and nefarious
        are our iniquities.

⁷ Our ancestors in Egypt failed
        to see God working there;
    And by the Red Sea they rebelled
        despite His love and care.

⁸ And yet the Lord protected them
        because they were His own;
    He showed the glory of His name
        and made His power known.

⁹ The Lord rebuked the foaming deep,
        exposing solid land;
    He led them through the Red Sea depths
        as if on desert sand.

¹⁰ The Lord preserved them from the sword
        and kept them in His sight;
    He rescued them from enemies
        and saved them from the fight.

¹¹ The Lord released the mighty waves
        that caught their foes in stride;
    The roaring sea came sweeping down,
        no enemy survived.

¹² Then Israel believed the Lord
        and trusted in His name;
    They knew He kept His promises
        so praised Him with acclaim.

¹³ But just as quickly they forgot
        the wonders He had wrought;
    They did not want His counseling,
        nor was His wisdom sought.

¹⁴ The Lord was tested thoroughly
    by their display of greed;
For in the desert they succumbed
    to every want and need.

¹⁵ At first the Lord gave what they asked
    so they would be appeased;
But then He let them waste away
    by sickness and disease.

¹⁶ To Moses' and to Aaron's rule,
    their jealousy arose;
Although the two obeyed the Lord
    and were the ones He chose.

¹⁷ The Lord's hand opened up the earth,
    devouring Dathan;
While relatives of Abiram
    were buried in the sand.

¹⁸ With raging fires burning wild
    that set their camp ablaze,
The ones who stood against the Lord
    were cut down for their ways.

¹⁹ They forged a calf near Horeb's slopes,
    an idol cast from gold,
Then worshiped what their hands had made,
    an object mute and cold.

²⁰ They turned from God and looked upon
    the image of an ox –
An animal that finds its food
    from grass among the rocks.

²¹ O they forgot to worship God
    Who'd kept them in His care,
And ransomed them from Egypt's hand
    when they were in despair.

22 The Lord had shown them miracles
    while Egypt bound them tight;
And when the Red Sea blocked their way,
    He showed His awesome might.

23 And so the Lord said they would die,
    but Moses took a stand;
He begged the Lord to stay His wrath,
    and God withheld His hand.

24 But then they did not like the land,
    despising it instead;
They did not put their hope in God
    or trust in what He said.

25 They grumbled loudly in their tents
    and would not be deterred;
They did not care to follow God
    or listen to His word.

26 The Lord then swore upon His oath,
    declaring His intent,
That in the desert they would die
    because of their dissent.

27 And their descendants would be thrown
    to nations far and wide,
Dispersed and scattered by the Lord
    to lands where they'd abide.

28 Yet still they worshipped Baal-Peor,
    and to its lies were wed;
They ate the pagan offerings
    presented to the dead.

29 They angered and provoked the Lord
    by all their wicked ways;
And so He struck them with a plague –
    a scourge to end their days.

³⁰ But Phinehas rebuked the vile
    by standing up unswayed;
By holding firm against their sin,
    the pestilence was stayed.

³¹ His action was attributed
    as one of righteousness,
A symbol for a future time
    to those who would regress.

³² Yet near the pool of Meribah,
    once more they sparked God's wrath;
And Moses tripped because of them
    and stumbled on his path.

³³ For there they turned against the Lord,
    His Spirit, and His way;
And many were the careless words
    that Moses spoke that day.

³⁴ God's people also did not kill
    the heathen in the land;
They did not act to strike them down
    as was the Lord's command.

³⁵ Instead, they mingled with the tribes
    and did not stay apart;
They learned the pagan practices,
    which tainted every heart.

³⁶ They worshipped idols carved from wood
    by offering a prayer;
They served these objects openly,
    which trapped them like a snare.

³⁷ They even offered up their sons
    and daughters to be slain;
They sacrificed them to their gods
    in horror and in vain.

³⁸ They practiced their idolatry
    and shed their children's blood,
Which desecrated Canaan's land
    like sewage in a flood.

³⁹ Their actions were despicable
    and left their souls defiled;
Like prostitutes they fouled themselves
    by deeds the Lord reviled.

⁴⁰ The Lord was angered by their acts,
    their arrogance and pride;
Abhorring His inheritance,
    His wrath would not subside.

⁴¹ The Lord released them to their foes
    who crushed them like a weight;
Their adversaries governed them
    and ruled them out of hate.

⁴² Their enemies were cruel to them,
    oppression was their plight;
They felt the power of the fist
    and grip that held them tight.

⁴³ Though many times God rescued them,
    rebellion was their way;
And so they sunk into their sin
    that made their souls decay.

⁴⁴ But still God loved them in distress,
    He listened to each sigh;
He saw their pain and misery,
    He heard His people cry.

⁴⁵ He thought about His covenant
    and of His loving care,
And so relented in His wrath
    to lift them from despair.

⁴⁶ And when the Lord was merciful,
    He let their plight be known;
He made their captives pity them
    and care about each groan.

⁴⁷ O Lord our God, come save us now
    from nations all around;
Then blessings to Your holy name
    and praises will abound.

⁴⁸ O praise the God of Israel,
    from age to age the same;
Let all the people say, *"Amen,"*
    and praise His holy name.

Psalm 107

¹ O praise the Lord, for He is good,
    His love will long endure;
Give thanks to Him and bless His name
    both now and evermore.

² Let those delivered by the Lord
    rejoice because they're free,
Declaring how He saved their lives
    from every enemy.

³ And let them tell how they were lost
    but how He called them forth,
Collecting them from east and west
    and lands both south and north.

⁴ Some wandered in the wilderness
    where desert creatures roam;
They found no place to settle down,
    no town to call a home.

⁵ They had no food for nourishment,
    no drink to quench their thirst;
Their strength and hopes were vanishing
    like those whose lives are cursed.

⁶ Amidst their trouble and distress,
    they cried out in alarm;
The Lord responded to their pleas
    and rescued them from harm.

⁷ The Lord directed them along
    by showing them the way;
He took them to a settlement,
    a place where they could stay.

⁸ O let them thank and praise the Lord
    for His unending love,
The wonders He has shown to them,
    His mercies from above.

⁹ The Lord has satisfied their thirst
    from ever flowing springs;
He's given meat and daily bread
    and food befitting kings.

¹⁰ Some languished in the murky dark
    with suffering and pains,
Like prisoners without a hope,
    in misery and chains.

¹¹ For they had not believed God's word,
    rejecting it instead;
They spurned the counsel of the Lord,
    ignoring what He said.

¹² God humbled them with drudgery
    as slaves upon the land;
They stumbled in their laboring
    without a helping hand.

¹³ Amidst their trouble and distress,
    they cried out in alarm;
The Lord responded to their pleas
    and rescued them from harm.

¹⁴ The Lord redeemed them from the gloom
    and shadows of the night;
He broke the fetters and the chains
    that bound and held them tight.

¹⁵ So let them show their gratitude
    and thank the Lord above;
For many wonders He has done
    by His unending love.

¹⁶ The Lord has shattered gates of bronze
    so they would not restrain;
He's cut through iron prison bars
    and broken every chain.

¹⁷ Yet some were fools and turned from God
    by their iniquities,
And paid for their rebelliousness
    by suffering disease.

¹⁸ They could not stand the sight of food,
    its odor choked their breath;
Their lives were passing from this world
    and to the gates of death.

¹⁹ Amidst their trouble and distress,
    they cried out in alarm;
The Lord responded to their pleas
    and rescued them from harm.

²⁰ The Lord spoke out a healing word
    to comfort and to save;
And by His might delivered them
    and snatched them from the grave.

²¹ So let them show their gratitude
    and thank the Lord above;
For many wonders He has done
    by His unending love.

²² O let them thank Him for His deeds
    and marvels of His ways,
And sing with joy while offering
    a sacrifice of praise.

²³ A few went to the sea in ships
    to sail before the breeze;
They plied the waters in their boats
    to trade upon the seas.

²⁴ They saw the wonders of the Lord
    across the ocean sweep,
His fabulous and mighty works
    and marvels of the deep.

²⁵ The Lord spoke sharply to the sea,
    the surf and waves grew high;
A mighty tempest swirled the foam
    that reached up to the sky.

²⁶ The ships were lifted heavenward
    and then came crashing down;
The sailors lost their bravery
    and feared that they would drown.

²⁷ They staggered much like drunken men
    who struggle just to stand;
Their skill was useless in the storm
    so far away from land.

²⁸ Amidst their trouble and distress,
    they cried out in alarm;
The Lord responded to their pleas
    and rescued them from harm.

²⁹ He stilled the tumult of the seas
    and bade the winds to cease;
He hushed the crashing of the waves
    till all lay still at peace.

³⁰ They celebrated how the Lord
    had calmed the churning deep;
And so He guided them to port,
    secure within His keep.

³¹ So let them show their gratitude
    and thank the Lord above;
For many wonders He has done
    by His unending love.

³² Let those assembled praise His name,
    let every shout repeat;
And let the hallelujahs ring
    wherever elders meet.

³³ The Lord slowed rivers to a craw
    till verdant land was browned;
He dried up all the flowing springs
    till cracks broke through the ground.

³⁴ The Lord turned fruitful earth to salt
    as dry as desert sand,
Because of all the wickedness
    and evil in the land.

³⁵ But then He changed it back again
    and made the rivers flow;
He turned the sands to bursting springs
    where living things could grow.

³⁶ The Lord gave hungry people hope
    and settled them with care;
They built a city for their own,
    a place beyond compare.

³⁷ They planted vineyards on the hills,
    sowed seed in every field;
They watched the fruit and grain grow ripe,
    then harvested its yield.

³⁸ The Lord poured blessings over them,
   and so they multiplied;
He watched the growing of their herds
   so they would not subside.

³⁹ But misery and sorrow struck,
   which left their hearts forlorn;
They suffered from adversity,
   disparagement and scorn.

⁴⁰ The Lord derided every prince
   and those who had command;
He made them wander aimlessly
   throughout a trackless land.

⁴¹ But He delivered those in want
   so they would be secure;
He grew their numbers like a flock,
   ensuring they'd endure.

⁴² And so the righteous celebrate
   these things they've seen and heard;
The wicked though are put to shame
   and do not speak a word.

⁴³ O let the wise consider this
   and ponder it with care,
Considering the Lord's great deeds
   and love beyond compare.

Psalm 108

¹ My heart is ever true, O God,
   my heart is ever true;
And I will sing the sweetest song
   to praise and worship You.

² Awake my soul and rise with me,
   awake O harp and strings;
For I will wake the dawning day
   as all creation sings.

³ O Lord, among the nations will
    I thank You all my days;
Among the people everywhere,
    I'll ever sing Your praise.

⁴ For greater is Your faithfulness
    than sun and stars above;
And higher still than heaven's throne
    is Your unfailing love.

⁵ So in the heavens show Your might,
    display Your strength on high;
And let Your glory fill the earth,
    the oceans, and the sky.

⁶ O Lord, reach down and rescue us
    by way of Your right hand;
Protect those whom You dearly love,
    who dwell within Your land.

⁷ For in the temple You once said,
    "I give to you this oath:
That I will portion Shechem's land
    and parcel out Succoth.

⁸ *For Gilead belongs to me,*
    Manasseh's my delight;
I've Judah's scepter for my rule
    and Ephraim as my might.

⁹ *But Moab is my washing bowl,*
    and Edom feels my shoe;
While over Philistia's tribes
    I'll shout with strength anew."

¹⁰ O who will go before me, Lord,
    to fortify my cause?
And who will guide me on the way
    that leads to Edom's walls?

¹¹ O Lord, have You rejected us?
    Do You not hear our pleas?
Will You not help our armies fight
    against our enemies?

¹² O help us in the battle, Lord,
    to crush those we oppose;
For human help has little worth
    and won't defeat our foes.

¹³ For You give us the victory
    and help us win the war;
You tread upon our enemy
    to make our triumph sure.

Psalm 109

¹ O God, You are the One I praise
    and worship every day;
Do not be silent anymore,
    but hear me when I pray.

² The wicked speak with evil tongues
    when spewing forth their lies,
Accusing me with every tale
    and falsehood they devise.

³ They come at me with hateful words
    without relief or pause,
Attacking me with cursing lips
    for no apparent cause.

⁴ They slander me relentlessly
    although I've been their friend;
And yet despite the things they do,
    my life of prayer won't end.

⁵ I've sought to do good things for them,
    but evil they return;
I've offered them the hand of peace,
    which angrily they spurn.

⁶ O Lord, select an evil judge
    to rule against my foes;
Appoint a liar to accuse
    and multiply their woes.

⁷ May they receive dishonest trials
    with verdicts that condemn;
May every prayer that they recite
    cause guilt to fall on them.

⁸ May they pass quickly from this life,
    not leaving any trace;
May they be spurned from leadership
    while others take their place.

⁹ May they be cursed with shattered homes
    and broken families,
Their spouse and children all alone
    and begging on their knees.

¹⁰ May they be crushed to contemplate
    their children who will roam,
And who will scrounge for daily needs
    when driven from their home.

¹¹ May they be plagued by creditors
    who seize their goods and lands;
May strangers plunder all they own –
    the labor of their hands.

¹² May they not hear a kindly word
    or feel another's care;
May no one show their children grace
    or lift them from despair.

¹³ May they have no inheritance,
    their future line erased;
May their descendants be cut off,
    their lineage displaced.

¹⁴ O may their fathers' sins and wrongs
  be known before the Lord;
And may their mothers' evil ways
  forever be abhorred.

¹⁵ And may the Lord declare their guilt
  for all their wicked ways,
So no one thinks of them again
  or recollects their days.

¹⁶ For they are not compassionate,
  the needy they oppress;
They persecute the destitute
  and kill those in distress.

¹⁷ May those who love to voice a curse
  be cursed by what they've said;
May those who hate to praise or bless
  be filled with fear and dread.

¹⁸ For cursing is a robe for them
  that covers up their soul;
It seeps into their inner parts
  like oil in a hole.

¹⁹ So may it choke the breath from them
  and bind them by its spite,
Like belts pulled close around their waists
  that squeeze and hold them tight.

²⁰ May this be how the Lord repays
  those falsely blaming me;
May those with evil on their tongues
  be shamed so all can see.

²¹ So come, O Lord, deliver me
  and help me from above;
And for the glory of Your name,
  protect me by Your love.

²² For I am poor and needy, Lord,
  my life is torn apart;
I'm greatly troubled and distressed
  and wounded in my heart.

²³ I fade away like eventide,
  a shadow in the night;
I fall like locusts in the wind,
  exhausted from their flight.

²⁴ My knees are weak from lack of food,
  I'm tired from my groans;
My body slowly wastes away
  till all that shows are bones.

²⁵ I feel the scorn of those who seek
  to tear my life to shreds;
Whenever I come near to them,
  they turn and shake their heads.

²⁶ So come, O Lord, deliver me
  and help me from above;
O save me by Your awesome grace
  according to Your love.

²⁷ O let my foes see how You save
  whenever I'm distressed;
Let no one doubt that it's Your hand
  by which my life is blessed.

²⁸ And though they curse and threaten me,
  Your love will see me through;
So let their lives be filled with shame
  while I rejoice in You.

²⁹ May everyone who slanders me
  be covered with disgrace;
May they be dressed in robes of shame
  with scandal as its lace.

³⁰ O I will ever thank the Lord,
    for awesome are His ways;
  Among the people that He loves,
    I'll lift His name in praise.

³¹ The Lord is close to those in need
    and watches over them;
  And He will surely save their lives
    from those who would condemn.

Psalm 110

¹ The Lord said to my lord and king,
    "Come near and take a seat,
Until I make your enemies
    a footstool for your feet."

² O king, the Lord will raise your rod,
    from Zion it will go;
  And you will rule your enemies
    and conquer every foe.

³ Your people will be sure to fight
    when you come into view;
  In holiness your youth are drawn
    and cling to you like dew.

⁴ The Lord has sworn a solemn pledge
    to make your future sure:
  "You are much like Melchizedek,
    a priest forevermore."

⁵ The Lord is always near to you
    and close to your right hand;
  His wrath will level mighty kings
    when He is in command.

⁶ The nations will be judged by Him
    according to their worth;
  He'll pile up corpses in the fields
    and smite the kings on earth.

7 And then, O king, you'll stop and drink
    from brooks that ripple by;
  And when your soul has been refreshed,
    you'll lift your head up high.

Psalm 111

1 With hallelujahs to the Lord,
    I'll thank Him all my days;
  And when the righteous gather round,
    I'll shout and sing His praise.

2 For great and awesome are the works
    and wonders of the Lord;
  They fill us with delight and joy
    when pondered and explored.

3 His deeds are truly marvelous,
    magnificent and grand;
  His righteousness is wonderful
    and will forever stand.

4 The Lord displays His miracles
    to press them on our mind;
  His hand is always merciful,
    compassionate and kind.

5 The Lord gives food and sustenance
    to those who fear His name;
  He won't forsake His covenant,
    from age to age the same.

6 The Lord has shown His chosen ones
    the power of His deeds;
  He's given them the nations' lands
    to satisfy their needs.

7 The Lord works wonders by His hands
    because His ways are just;
  His precepts are reliable
    to follow and to trust.

8 The Lord creates His mighty works
  so they will long endure;
He fashions them in faithfulness
  to be forever pure.

9 The Lord ordained His covenant
  and set His people free;
His name is worthy of all praise,
  the holy One is He.

10 To fear the Lord will make us wise
  and help us know His ways;
So always follow His commands,
  and ever give Him praise.

Psalm 112

1 The Lord will bless and honor those
  who worship Him with awe,
Those singing praises to His name,
  delighting in His law.

2 Their children will experience
  the blessings of His hand;
And they'll be called the mighty ones,
  the upright in the land.

3 Their households will be prosperous
  with wealth for all to see;
Their righteousness will brightly shine
  for all eternity.

4 And even in the darkest gloom,
  they'll see a dawning light,
Because they are compassionate
  and do what's just and right.

5 And surely they will be at peace
  and always be secure,
Because they lend what they possess
  and keep their actions pure.

⁶ The righteous will not trip or fall
or ever be disgraced;
The memory of them will last
and never be erased.

⁷ Distressing news won't trouble them
or tear their lives apart,
Because they trust upon the Lord
and keep a steadfast heart.

⁸ They rest contented without fear,
with no concerns or woes;
For they will have the victory
and overcome their foes.

⁹ They lavish gifts on those in want,
responding to each cry;
Their righteousness will long endure,
their honor lifted high.

¹⁰ The wicked will be vexed to see
the virtuous prevail;
They'll gnash their teeth then disappear
as their desires fail.

Psalm 113

¹ O praise the Lord and worship Him
with honor and acclaim;
O come now servants of the Lord
and praise His holy name.

² Yes, come and bless the Lord our God
and let Your voices soar;
Give thanks to Him and praise His name
both now and evermore.

³ From dawning light that greets the day
until the setting sun,
The Lord will hear His holy name
be praised by everyone.

4 He rules the nations far below
    from where He reigns on high;
His glory shines above the stars,
    the heavens and the sky.

5 O who is like the Lord our God,
    the One of greatest worth,
Who sits and reigns within the heights,
    enthroned above the earth?

6 And who but God will bend their back
    while seeking to behold,
The heavens and the earth beneath,
    and all the things they hold?

7 The Lord cares deeply for the poor
    and lifts them by His hand;
He pulls them from a gloomy pit
    of ash and sinking sand.

8 The Lord puts them where princes dwell
    and has them take a seat;
With princes of the ones He loves,
    is where they'll rest their feet.

9 O praise the Lord Who hears the cries
    of women all alone;
He makes them happy with the gift
    of children of their own.

Psalm 114

1 When Israel fled Egypt's rule
    the way the Lord had planned,
And Jacob made the exodus
    and left that foreign land –

2 Then Judah rose as God's elect,
    a nation where He'd reign;
And Israel became His own
    dominion and domain.

3 The Red Sea split before the Lord
   as winds began to blow;
The Jordan River stopped its course
   and promptly changed its flow.

4 The mountains skipped like frightened sheep
   and jumped about like rams;
The hills rebelled like skittish ewes
   and shied away like lambs.

5 So tell us, Sea, why did you split
   and waters open wide?
And why, O Jordan, did your flow
   reverse like ebbing tide?

6 And why, O mountains, did you shake
   and jump about like rams?
And why, O hills, were you upset
   and shy away like lambs?

7 O tremble, earth, before the Lord
   when He is drawing near;
O when the God of Jacob comes,
   be filled with awe and fear.

8 For God turned rock into a spring –
   an overflowing pool,
From solid rock to quenching spring
   that sparkled fresh and cool.

Psalm 115

1 O not to us, Lord, not to us,
   but to You be the fame;
Because You love us faithfully,
   we glorify Your name.

2 Why do the nations taunt us, Lord:
   "Where is your God today?
   Why do you never hear from Him?
   Why does He stay away?"

3 Our God's in heaven high above,
    beyond the earth and sun;
He does whatever pleases Him,
    the things that He wants done.

4 But pagans worship idols cast
    from silver ore and gold;
Mere human hands have fashioned them
    inanimate and cold.

5 They have an open mouth, but yet
    are silent as the night;
They've eyes that stare out into space
    but don't have any sight.

6 They have two ears for listening
    but cannot hear a prayer;
They have a nose for drawing breath
    but cannot breathe the air.

7 They have two legs with feet and toes
    but cannot walk around;
Their hands can never touch or feel,
    their throats can't make a sound.

8 Their makers will become like them
    and thus will end their days;
And so will those who trust in them
    and follow in their ways.

9 So come now trust upon the Lord,
    O house of Israel,
The Lord who is your help and shield
    and comes to make you well.

10 And come now trust upon the Lord,
    O you of Aaron's seed,
The Lord who is your help and shield
    and meets your every need.

¹¹ Yes, come now trust upon the Lord,
    O you who fear His name,
  The Lord who is your help and shield
    and evermore the same.

¹² The Lord will long remember us
    with blessings for our way;
  He'll bless the tribes of Israel
    and Aaron every day.

¹³ The Lord will bless those bowing low
    in reverence and awe,
  And those who fear and honor Him,
    no matter great or small.

¹⁴ So may the Lord be kind to you
    and see to your increase;
  May all your heirs be plentiful,
    your lineage not cease.

¹⁵ O may the Lord be kind to you
    with blessings from His hand;
  For He made heaven and the earth
    by word of His command.

¹⁶ The highest heavens are the Lord's,
    from there He'll always reign;
  But He has given us the earth
    to rule as our domain.

¹⁷ The Lord wants worship from our lips,
    the dead can't give Him praise;
  For those who lie within the ground
    can't thank Him for His ways.

¹⁸ So let's rejoice and praise the Lord
    and let our voices soar;
  Let's bless Him with the songs we sing
    both now and evermore.

Psalm 116

¹ I love the Lord and honor Him
   because He knows my cry;
 I give Him thanks for listening
   and hearing every sigh.

² Because He hearkens to my voice
   and turns His ear to me,
 I'll call on Him while I'm alive
   and lift to Him my plea.

³ For once I knew the grip of death
   and terror of the grave,
 When sorrow and anxiety
   engulfed me like a wave.

⁴ But then I called upon the Lord
   from deep within that hole;
 I cried that He would rescue me
   and save my frightened soul.

⁵ The Lord is merciful and kind
   and helps us like a friend;
 His righteousness will long endure,
   His goodness has no end.

⁶ The Lord protects the innocent
   by watching from above;
 He saw me in my helplessness
   and saved me by His love.

⁷ So be at rest, my anguished heart,
   O be reposed, my soul,
 Because the Lord takes perfect care
   to make the spirit whole.

⁸ The Lord delivered me from death
   and wiped away my tears;
 He kept my feet from staggering
   and banished all my fears.

⁹ And so I walk before the Lord,
  secure within His hand,
Alive and glad to be with those
  who dwell within the land.

¹⁰ I kept on hoping in the Lord,
  believing in His might,
Although afflicted and distressed
  and fearing for my plight.

¹¹ When agitated and alarmed,
  I cried out in disgust,
"All people lie and plan deceit,
  there's no one I can trust."

¹² Is there a sacrifice to give
  or something I can do,
To pay the Lord for how His grace
  restored my life anew?

¹³ I'll thank the Lord for saving me
  by giving Him acclaim;
I'll bring Him offerings of wine
  and call upon His name.

¹⁴ Before His people I will stand
  when I have been restored;
And there I'll keep my covenant,
  my promise to the Lord.

¹⁵ O truly precious to the Lord
  is any saint who dies;
It troubles Him when those He loves
  encounter their demise.

¹⁶ O Lord, I always honor You
  by serving faithfully;
I serve You as my mother did,
  and You have set me free.

¹⁷ I call upon Your name, O Lord,
    when lifting up my prayer –
An offering of thanks to You
    because of how You care.

¹⁸ Before Your people I will stand
    when I have been restored;
And there I'll keep my covenant,
    my promise to You, Lord.

¹⁹ Yes, in Your temple courts I'll keep
    the pledges that I gave;
I'll praise You in Jerusalem
    because, O Lord, You save.

Psalm 117

¹ O praise the Lord and worship Him
    with honor and acclaim;
All people of the nations shout
    and glorify His name.

² For He will always care for us
    through His amazing love;
His faithfulness will long endure,
    so praise the Lord above.

Psalm 118

¹ O thank the Lord for He is good,
    His righteousness is sure;
His love abides eternally,
    enduring evermore.

² O come now Israel and say
    of Him whom you adore,
"His love abides eternally,
    enduring evermore."

3 O come now those of Aaron's house,
   and let your hearts implore,
"His love abides eternally,
   enduring evermore."

4 And come now all who fear the Lord,
   and sing with hearts that soar,
"His love abides eternally,
   enduring evermore."

5 When in distress I begged the Lord
   to listen to my plea;
And he responded to my cry
   and set my spirit free.

6 The Lord is ever close to me
   so I need never fear;
What can another do to me
   as long as God is near?

7 The Lord is ever close to me,
   a help in time of need;
So I can face my enemies
   with courage to proceed.

8 Far better to depend on God,
   to trust upon the Lord,
Than seek protection and the help
   that others can accord.

9 Far better to depend on God,
   to trust upon the Lord,
Than look to kings and royalty
   for help to be restored.

10 The nations all surrounded me,
   destruction was their aim;
But by the power of the Lord,
   I crushed them in His name.

¹¹ Yes, nations circled all around,
　　from every side they came;
And by the power of the Lord,
　　I crushed them in His name.

¹² They struck at me like swarming bees,
　　then flickered like a flame;
Yet by the power of the Lord,
　　I crushed them in His name.

¹³ In battle they had pushed me back
　　until I nearly fell;
But then the Lord assisted me
　　to keep me safe and well.

¹⁴ The Lord's become my saving grace,
　　the One who makes me strong;
He lifted me when I was down,
　　and gave my heart this song.

¹⁵ With joyfulness within their tents,
　　the righteous shout and sing;
Because the right hand of the Lord
　　has done a mighty thing.

¹⁶ The right hand of the Lord is raised,
　　preparing for the fight;
The valiant right hand of the Lord
　　comes down with force and might.

¹⁷ O surely now I will not die,
　　but I will live restored;
And so I'll tell about the works
　　and wonders of the Lord.

¹⁸ Although the Lord has punished me,
　　He's sheltered me from death;
And though I've tasted His rebuke,
　　my body still has breath.

^{19} So open up the temple courts,
    the gates of righteousness;
So I can enter praising God
    to worship and to bless.

^{20} This is the gate the Lord has made,
    it's closed to those who sin,
The gate through which the righteous walk,
    the gate they enter in.

^{21} I thank the Lord for listening
    and answering my plea;
For He is my salvation now,
    my joy and victory.

^{22} The stone rejected in the plan
    became the cornerstone;
The one the builders cast aside
    became the one that shone.

^{23} The Lord has done these awesome things
    because He's good and wise;
How wonderful that we should see
    these marvels with our eyes.

^{24} Today's the day the Lord has made,
    let everyone rejoice;
Let's gladly lift our hearts to sing
    and praise Him with one voice.

^{25} O save us, Lord, and give us help,
    and do not let us fail;
But let us savor victory
    when we alone prevail.

^{26} O may God bless the one who comes
    in our Lord's holy name;
For from His courts we honor you
    with blessings we proclaim.

27 The Lord is God, He gives us light,
  so join the festive throng;
And march around the altar horns
  with boughs you bring along.

28 For You, O Lord, are my true God,
  the One that I pursue;
I'll sing Your praises all my days
  and ever worship You.

29 O thank the Lord for He is good,
  His righteousness is sure;
His love abides eternally,
  enduring evermore.

Psalm 119

1 How happy those whose lives are pure
  and faultless in their ways,
Who walk according to God's law
  and keep it all their days.

2 How happy those who know His word
  and from it won't depart,
And who are ever seeking Him
  with all their mind and heart.

3 They never choose an evil path
  or actions that are wrong,
But always follow in His ways
  by walking close along.

4 O Lord, the precepts You ordained
  and carefully conveyed,
Are to be fully carried out
  and perfectly obeyed.

5 O how I long for faithfulness
  to keep Your statutes true;
I yearn that I could mold my ways
  to always follow You.

⁶ For I would never be ashamed
    or know a reprimand,
  As long as I would meditate
    on all that You command.

⁷ And I will praise You with my heart
    and sing with great delight,
  When learning of Your noble laws
    and judgments that are right.

⁸ O I will keep Your statutes, Lord
    and closely guard Your law;
  So don't forsake or turn from me,
    don't let me trip and fall.

• • •

⁹ O Lord, how can the young be good
    and keep their habits pure?
  It's only living by Your word
    their way will be secure.

¹⁰ With all my heart I seek You out
    to faithfully obey;
  So help me follow Your commands
    that I will never stray.

¹¹ I prize the word You've given me
    and saved it in my heart;
  So I won't sin against You, Lord,
    or from Your word depart.

¹² O Lord, I bless and honor You,
    exalting You with praise;
  Instruct and teach me Your decrees,
    and guide me in Your ways.

¹³ I speak to those from east and west
    and people north and south,
  About the judgments You've revealed
    and uttered from Your mouth.

¹⁴ Your testimonies are a joy
       and lovely to behold;
   To me they're far more beautiful
       than precious gems or gold.

¹⁵ I keep Your precepts ever close
       to meditate upon;
   I ponder deeply all Your ways
       and contemplate each one.

¹⁶ Your statutes fill me with delight,
       they're pleasant and refined;
   Your law will not escape by heart
       or ever leave my mind.

• • •

¹⁷ Be kind to me, your servant, Lord,
       so that my heart is spurred,
   To live in strict obedience
       according to Your word.

¹⁸ Come open up my eyes to see
       and fill my mind with awe;
   That I may know how wonderful
       and lovely is Your law.

¹⁹ As I am merely passing through,
       a stranger on the earth;
   Do not conceal Your just decrees,
       but let me know their worth.

²⁰ My soul is longing for Your laws
       and all that You command;
   While thoughts of them consume my mind,
       which tries to understand.

²¹ You reprimand those filled with pride,
       the arrogant and vain,
   Those disobeying Your commands
       and words that You ordain.

²² But I have kept Your statutes, Lord,
    so shelter me from scorn;
Deliver me from all contempt
    so I am not forlorn.

²³ Though princes sit and slander me
    by saying what they please,
My mind will always meditate
    and study Your decrees.

²⁴ Your testimonies have become
    my joy and great delight,
My ever-present counselors
    that show the way that's right.

• • •

²⁵ My soul is crushed and beaten down
    and holding onto dust;
Revive me as You promised, Lord,
    for in Your word I trust.

²⁶ Since I've accounted for my ways,
    and You have answered me,
Instruct me how to comprehend
    the statutes You decree.

²⁷ Explain to me Your precepts, Lord,
    so I can understand;
Then I will think about the works
    and wonders from Your hand.

²⁸ My soul is crushed by grief and woe,
    my spirit is deterred;
So come, O Lord, and strengthen me
    according to Your word.

²⁹ O lead me from the wayward path
    and all deceitful ways;
Instruct me closely in Your law
    to guide me all my days.

³⁰ My heart has chosen faithfulness
 to follow after You;
 I've placed Your laws in front of me
 for what they teach is true.

³¹ I love Your testimonies, Lord,
 to keep them is my aim;
 So do not let me be disgraced
 or ever put to shame.

³² I'll run the way of Your commands
 and things You ask of me,
 Because You have enlarged my heart
 and set my spirit free.

• • •

³³ Instruct me in Your statutes, Lord,
 that I may comprehend;
 Then I will follow where they lead
 and keep them to the end.

³⁴ O give me understanding, Lord,
 so I'll observe Your laws,
 Obeying them with all my heart
 no matter what befalls.

³⁵ Direct me on the narrow path
 by doing what is right;
 For Your commandments give me joy
 and fill me with delight.

³⁶ Incline my heart to following
 Your testimonies, Lord;
 Don't let me want dishonest gain
 or seek unjust reward.

³⁷ Direct my eyes from wickedness
 and things that make me stray;
 Deliver and preserve my life
 according to Your way.

³⁸ O Lord, uphold Your covenant,
    the promise made to me,
So You'll be held in reverence
    by all who look and see.

³⁹ Protect me from the shame I dread
    and insults that I fear;
And let me know Your judgments, Lord,
    so good and ever near.

⁴⁰ O how I need Your precepts, Lord,
    so I will not transgress;
Revive and keep me through Your grace,
    and by Your righteousness.

• • •

⁴¹ O show me Your salvation, Lord,
    Your never-ending love;
Come save me by Your spoken word
    and promise from above.

⁴² Then I can answer when I'm scorned
    and when my name is slurred;
I'll stand against each taunt and wound
    because I trust Your word.

⁴³ Empower me to speak the truth
    whenever I'm in need,
Because I trust Your judgments, Lord,
    and laws that You've decreed.

⁴⁴ I'll carefully obey Your law
    because it's good and pure,
While keeping it most faithfully
    for now and evermore.

⁴⁵ I'll live in perfect liberty
    and freely walk about;
For I obey Your precepts, Lord,
    and always seek them out.

⁴⁶ Your testimonies I'll proclaim
    to princes and to kings;
  I will not be ashamed to speak
    and tell about such things.

⁴⁷ For Your commandments bring me joy
    and fill me with delight;
  I love to follow in Your way,
    the path that's good and right.

⁴⁸ I raise my hands to Your commands
    because I love each one;
  And every statute that You give,
    I meditate upon.

• • •

⁴⁹ Recall Your promise made to me,
    Your faithful servant, Lord;
  It's strengthened me with hopefulness
    and left my soul restored.

⁵⁰ Though suffering adversity
    and torn apart by strife,
  Your promise has encouraged me,
    Your word has given life.

⁵¹ The arrogant keep taunting me
    with words to crush my heart;
  Yet I am steadfast to Your law,
    and from it won't depart.

⁵² I think about Your judgments, Lord,
    the ones from ancient days;
  They comfort like a soothing balm,
    relieving my malaise.

⁵³ But when the vile forsake Your law
    and turn instead to sin,
  My soul rebels at what it sees,
    my anger burns within.

⁵⁴ Your statutes never leave my mind
    but fill me like a song,
A song to sing if I'm at rest
    or traveling along.

⁵⁵ I hold Your name before me, Lord,
    all day and through the night;
I keep Your law and follow it
    because it's good and right.

⁵⁶ For this has been how I have lived,
    the order of my day –
To listen to Your precepts, Lord,
    to hear them and obey.

• • •

⁵⁷ Lord, You're my portion in this life,
    the One for whom I thirst;
I've promised to uphold Your words
    and always keep them first.

⁵⁸ To know the favor of Your grace
    has been my heartfelt prayer;
So by the promise of Your word,
    extend Your loving care.

⁵⁹ I've contemplated how I live
    and thought about my ways;
The testimonies that You give
    will guide me all my days.

⁶⁰ And thus I hurry to comply,
    to act without delay,
To hold to Your commandments, Lord,
    to follow and obey.

⁶¹ Although the wicked bind me up
    with ropes that cut me raw,
Still, I will walk in faithfulness
    and not forsake Your law.

⁶² O I will rise and thank You, Lord,
    upon the dead of night,
Because Your righteous judgments shine
    more brightly than the light.

⁶³ And I will be a friend to those
    who fear and honor You,
To all who keep Your precepts, Lord,
    and to Your way are true.

⁶⁴ Your mercy fills the earth, O Lord,
    with love and grace for all;
Reveal and teach me Your decrees
    so I will never fall.

• • •

⁶⁵ I thank You as Your servant, Lord,
    for good things You bestow,
According to the word You gave
    and promised long ago.

⁶⁶ O teach me knowledge and to judge
    to help me understand;
For I have placed my hope and trust
    in all that You command.

⁶⁷ Before oppressed by suffering
    I wandered far astray;
But now I listen to Your word
    and carefully obey.

⁶⁸ O You are merciful and good,
    and what is right, You do;
So teach me Your commandments, Lord,
    and how to follow You.

⁶⁹ Although the arrogant tell lies
    that leave my name maligned,
Still Your instructions I will keep
    with all my heart and mind.

⁷⁰ The wicked are insensitive,
　　their hearts are mean and raw;
But I find joy and take delight
　　in teachings of Your law.

⁷¹ The suffering that I endured
　　was valuable for me,
Because I learned to follow You
　　and all that You decree.

⁷² O Lord, the law that's from Your mouth
　　is lovely to behold;
It's precious and more valuable
　　than silver coins or gold.

• • •

⁷³ O Lord, You have created me
　　and formed me with Your hands;
So help me understand Your laws
　　and follow Your commands.

⁷⁴ The righteous see me and rejoice,
　　their hearts within are stirred,
Because I've put my confidence
　　and hope upon Your word.

⁷⁵ O Lord, I know Your laws are right
　　and faithful is Your way;
So I can trust Your discipline
　　when I have gone astray.

⁷⁶ O show compassion for my life
　　by Your unfailing love;
According to Your promises,
　　give comfort from above.

⁷⁷ Display Your tender mercies, Lord,
　　that I may turn out right;
Because the law that comes from You
　　has been my heart's delight.

⁷⁸ O let the arrogant be shamed
    for wrongly hurting me;
And I will think and meditate
    on precepts You decree.

⁷⁹ May those who know Your statutes, Lord,
    who fear and honor You,
Be guided when they turn their eyes
    to see the things I do.

⁸⁰ Lord, help me ponder Your decrees
    and keep them in my heart;
So I will never be ashamed
    or from Your truth depart.

• • •

⁸¹ I long for Your salvation, Lord,
    from deep within my soul;
Your word is where I put my hope
    and trust to make me whole.

⁸² I look to find Your promises
    from eyes that barely see;
I cry out in my weariness,
    "When will You comfort me?"

⁸³ I'm like a wineskin in the smoke
    that's cracked and split apart;
Yet I recall Your statutes, Lord,
    and keep them in my heart.

⁸⁴ O how much longer must I wait?
    How long must I contend?
How long until Your judgment falls
    on those who seek my end?

⁸⁵ The arrogant have set their traps
    to make me trip and fall;
By this they disobey Your rules
    and violate Your law.

⁸⁶ But Your commands have always been
    reliable and true;
  So when the wicked trouble me
    I put my trust in You.

⁸⁷ And though the wicked seek to strike
    and wipe me from the land,
  I do not spurn or turn away
    from precepts You command.

⁸⁸ Revive me by Your kindness, Lord,
    and love that You provide;
  So testimonies that You give
    will always be my guide.

• • •

⁸⁹ Eternal is Your word, O Lord,
    it always will endure;
  It's fixed in heaven high above
    and stands forevermore.

⁹⁰ Your faithfulness from age to age
    will never pass away;
  For by Your hand You set the earth
    where it remains today.

⁹¹ And by Your ordinances, Lord,
    this will not slip from view;
  For everything that You have made
    will serve and honor You.

⁹² O if Your law had not been sweet
    and given me delight,
  I surely would have breathed my last,
    despairing of my plight.

⁹³ I won't forget Your precepts, Lord,
    but keep them in my heart;
  For by them You have rescued me
    and set my life apart.

⁹⁴ And since my life depends on You,
    salvation is my plea;
For I have sought Your precepts, Lord,
    and followed each decree.

⁹⁵ The wicked seek to take my life
    from where they lie in wait;
Yet on Your testimonies, Lord
    I'll ever meditate.

⁹⁶ All things I see are limited,
    there's nothing without flaw;
But Your commands are infinite,
    and perfect is Your law.

• • •

⁹⁷ O how I love Your law, O Lord,
    and cherish each decree;
Throughout the day I meditate
    on what they mean to me.

⁹⁸ I cling to Your commandments, Lord,
    and all that they disclose;
They make me know so many things
    and wiser than my foes.

⁹⁹ I meditate upon Your law,
    the statutes You command;
I've learned much more that those who teach
    will ever understand.

¹⁰⁰ I know what elders do not know,
    the things to which they're blind;
For I obey Your precepts, Lord,
    and let them fill my mind.

¹⁰¹ I've kept my feet from evil paths,
    avoiding wicked deeds;
I seek to know and keep Your law
    and follow where it leads.

¹⁰² I've never strayed from Your commands
　　or wandered from Your word;
　For You Yourself have taught these things,
　　and I have surely heard.

¹⁰³ How wonderful Your words, O Lord,
　　how sweet they are to me,
　Much sweeter to my open mouth
　　than honey from the bee.

¹⁰⁴ It's through Your precepts I have learned
　　the way that wisdom's gained;
　And thus I hate the evil ways
　　that You have not ordained.

• • •

¹⁰⁵ Your word's a lamp to guide my feet,
　　a light to show the way;
　O Lord, it shines upon my path
　　so I don't go astray.

¹⁰⁶ The solemn oath I pledge to You,
　　the promise I profess,
　Is that I'll closely keep Your laws,
　　Your rules of righteousness.

¹⁰⁷ But now I'm weak from suffering
　　and pray that You'll be stirred;
　Revive me, Lord, and give me life
　　according to Your word.

¹⁰⁸ Accept the offerings I bring,
　　my words and songs of praise;
　Instruct me in Your judgments, Lord,
　　direct me in Your ways.

¹⁰⁹ No matter where I turn there's risk
　　and danger to befall;
　Yet I will not forget to live
　　according to Your law.

¹¹⁰ The wicked seek to trip me up
    by laying out a snare;
  But I have kept Your precepts near
    so I will not despair.

¹¹¹ Your statutes are my heritage
    for now and evermore;
  They fill my heart with happiness
    and joy that will endure.

¹¹² I've fixed my heart upon Your laws
    to follow and comply;
  Obeying them is what I'll do
    until the day I die.

• • •

¹¹³ I hate whoever wavers, Lord,
    not giving You their all;
  But I delight in Your commands
    and love to keep Your law.

¹¹⁴ O Lord, You are my hiding place,
    my shelter and my shield;
  I put my hope upon Your word,
    and to it I will yield.

¹¹⁵ O sinners, get away from me
    and hastily depart;
  So the commandments of my God
    will dwell within my heart.

¹¹⁶ Sustain me, Lord, that I may live
    as promised by Your word;
  And do not let my hopes be dashed
    or spirit be deterred.

¹¹⁷ Uphold and firmly strengthen me
    so I will be secure;
  Then all Your statutes I'll respect
    for now and evermore.

¹¹⁸ O You reject the ones who stray
  and scoff at Your decrees;
For their deceit does not avail,
  nor do their lies appease.

¹¹⁹ You toss the wicked out like dross,
  like dregs upon the earth;
And thus I keep Your statutes close
  while treasuring their worth.

¹²⁰ My body trembles at Your name,
  I stand in reverent awe;
I'm fearful of Your judgments, Lord,
  and power of Your law.

• • •

¹²¹ O Lord, I've done what's good and just
  and lived by righteousness;
Do not abandon me to those
  who burden and oppress.

¹²² O give assurance of Your help
  that I will be all right;
Don't let the vile and arrogant
  exploit me by their might.

¹²³ My eyes are weak from keeping watch
  for Your salvation, Lord,
And longing for Your righteous word
  that all will be restored.

¹²⁴ So show me grace and kindliness
  according to Your love;
Explain and teach me Your decrees,
  reveal them from above.

¹²⁵ Because I am Your servant, Lord,
  please help me understand,
The testimonies You reveal,
  the way of each command.

¹²⁶ The time has come for You to act
and let Your judgment fall;
For many people disregard
and violate Your law.

¹²⁷ But I delight in Your commands,
they're lovely to behold,
More beautiful than precious stones,
more valuable than gold.

¹²⁸ O I esteem Your precepts Lord,
which show the way that's right;
But I despise a path that's wrong,
a trail that has no light.

• • •

¹²⁹ O Lord, Your testimonies shine,
they make the broken whole;
Because they are so wonderful,
I keep them in my soul.

¹³⁰ The right unfolding of Your words
turns darkness into light;
It pours out wisdom on the meek
and shows the way that's right.

¹³¹ I open up my mouth and pant
with yearning for Your word;
I long for Your commandments, Lord,
because my heart is stirred.

¹³² O turn Your face and look at me,
have mercy from above;
O bless me as You do for those
who lift Your name in love.

¹³³ And let Your word direct my steps
and guide them carefully;
Protect me from iniquities
so they don't master me.

¹³⁴ Redeem me from oppression, Lord,
    that comes from evil hands;
So I may follow Your decrees,
    Your precepts and commands.

¹³⁵ O make Your face shine full on me
    that I may see it glow;
Instruct me in Your statutes, Lord,
    to guide the way I go.

¹³⁶ O Lord, my tears are like a stream
    whose flow will not be stayed,
Because Your law is spurned by all
    and widely disobeyed.

• • •

¹³⁷ O Lord, You are the righteous One
    in Whom we put our trust;
Your judgments are correct and fair,
    Your laws are good and just.

¹³⁸ The testimonies You command
    in righteousness are fair;
Each one is born in faithfulness,
    there's none that can compare.

¹³⁹ A passion burns within my soul
    for greatly I'm disturbed,
Because my enemies have spurned
    and failed to heed Your word.

¹⁴⁰ O Your commands are beautiful,
    Your promises are pure;
And I, Your servant, cherish them,
    for they will long endure.

¹⁴¹ Although I'm small and timorous
    and thoroughly despised,
I won't forget Your precepts, Lord,
    to me they're highly prized.

¹⁴² Your righteousness will always last,
　　it's old but yet it's new;
　Your teachings are correct and sure,
　　Your law is ever true.

¹⁴³ Distress and trouble come at me,
　　I'm overwhelmed by fright;
　Yet Your commandments are my joy,
　　my hope and my delight.

¹⁴⁴ Your testimonies will remain
　　because they're good, O Lord;
　O help me understand each one
　　that I may live restored.

• • •

¹⁴⁵ O Lord, I cry with all my heart
　　that You would hear me pray;
　Then all Your statutes I will keep,
　　and Your commands obey.

¹⁴⁶ I cry aloud that You would come
　　to save and set me free;
　So testimonies that You give
　　will be observed by me.

¹⁴⁷ O I arise before the dawn
　　when day has not yet stirred;
　I pray that You will listen, Lord,
　　I hope upon Your word.

¹⁴⁸ I lie awake throughout the night
　　though it is dark and late;
　I think about Your promises
　　and on them meditate.

¹⁴⁹ O listen closely to my voice
　　by Your eternal love;
　Revive me by Your mercy, Lord,
　　and judgment from above.

150 The wicked come with evil schemes
        that fill me with dismay;
    For they are strangers to Your law,
        to them it's far away.

151 But You are ever near to me,
        there's none as close as You;
    And Your commandments will remain
        because Your word is true.

152 Your testimonies I have known
        and understood from old;
    For You, O Lord, created them
        to last till time untold.

• • •

153 Consider my afflictions, Lord,
        and troubles that befall;
    For though I'm plagued by suffering,
        I've not forgot Your law.

154 Defend my cause and plead my case,
        O come and set me free;
    According to the word You give,
        revive and rescue me.

155 The wicked will not be redeemed,
        they will not know Your grace;
    For they despise Your statutes, Lord,
        not one do they embrace.

156 But Your compassion is immense,
        Your mercies new each day;
    Preserve me by the laws You give
        according to Your way.

157 While many are my enemies
        who press from every side,
    The testimonies that You give
        remain my constant guide.

¹⁵⁸ I loathe the vile and treacherous,
    those faithless and untrue,
Because they have not kept Your word
    or followed after You.

¹⁵⁹ O how I love Your precepts, Lord,
    each word that You decree;
So by Your awesome grace and love,
    revive and rescue me.

¹⁶⁰ O Lord, Your word is always true,
    dependable and sure;
The righteous judgments that You give
    forever will endure.

• • •

¹⁶¹ Though kings and princes threaten me
    without excuse or cause,
O Lord, my heart attends to You
    and trembles at Your laws.

¹⁶² For I rejoice to hear Your word
    and promises from old,
Like one who finds a treasure trove
    of precious gems and gold.

¹⁶³ I hate dishonesty and lies
    and all that's not sincere;
But I rejoice and love Your law
    and always hold it dear.

¹⁶⁴ O seven times a day I come
    to offer up my praise,
To thank You for Your judgments, Lord,
    Your good and righteous ways.

¹⁶⁵ For those who ever love Your law
    have peace to fill each day;
There's nothing that can make them trip
    or stumble on their way.

¹⁶⁶ O I await the victory
    and Your salvation, Lord;
  For Your commands I've followed close,
    not one have I ignored.

¹⁶⁷ Your testimonies I have kept
    and planted in my soul;
  I love them all exceedingly
    because they make me whole.

¹⁶⁸ O Lord, I'm faithful to Your law,
    and to Your way I'm true;
  For everything I say and do
    is always known to You.

• • •

¹⁶⁹ O let my cry come near to You,
    and let my voice be heard;
  Provide me understanding, Lord,
    according to Your word.

¹⁷⁰ O let my supplication rise
    so You will hear its plea;
  According to Your promises,
    protect and rescue me.

¹⁷¹ My soul will ever worship You,
    my lips shall sing Your praise;
  For You have taught me Your decrees
    and versed me in Your ways.

¹⁷² O I shall sing about Your word
    and promises I trust;
  For the commandments You decree
    are virtuous and just.

¹⁷³ Forever be prepared to reach
    and help me with Your hand;
  For I observe Your precepts, Lord,
    and all that You command.

¹⁷⁴ I long that You would rescue me,
   I yearn to see things right;
   I'm filled with gladness by your law,
   and in it find delight.

¹⁷⁵ O let me live that I might praise
   and ever worship You;
   And let Your judgments guide my steps
   to stay the course that's true.

¹⁷⁶ O I have wandered like a sheep,
   so search for me today;
   For I know Your commandments, Lord,
   I've not forgot Your way.

Psalm 120

¹ I call upon the Lord my God
   when troubled and distressed;
   He listens and responds to me
   so I am greatly blessed.

² So come, O Lord, deliver me,
   redeem my soul I cry;
   Protect me from deceitful tongues
   and evil lips that lie.

³ But O deceitful tongues beware!
   For what is your reward?
   O what will be the punishment
   inflicted by the Lord?

⁴ For He will let His arrows fly
   and pierce you for your deeds;
   With red hot coals of juniper,
   you'll burn like withered weeds.

⁵ O woe is me for lingering
   in Meshech's far off land;
   For like the Kedar where I've dwelled,
   the wicked have command.

⁶ Yes I have lived with them too long,
    my soul demands release;
For they are savage in their ways
    and hate the thought of peace.

⁷ When I decry hostility,
    they answer with a roar;
The more I speak of love and peace,
    the more they cry for war.

Psalm 121

¹ I lift my eyes unto the hills,
    to mountains far away;
O where will help and aid come from
    to rescue me today?

² My help comes from the Lord Most High,
    the One of greatest worth,
Who fashioned heaven high above,
    Creator of the earth.

³ The Lord won't let you slip or fall
    but sees that you are blessed;
For He who watches over you
    won't slumber or take rest.

⁴ Indeed, the Lord Who reigns on high
    and watches Israel,
Won't slumber or recline to sleep,
    ensuring all is well.

⁵ The Lord protects and watches you
    and keeps you in His eye;
The Lord is shade at your right hand
    a covering on high.

⁶ The sun won't hurt you while it's day
    or blind you by its light;
Nor will the moon imperil you
    when day gives way to night.

⁷ The Lord secures you from all harm
     so you need never fear;
  He watches and defends your soul
     and keeps you ever near.

⁸ The Lord will watch you come and go,
     on this you can be sure;
  And He'll protect you on your way
     both now and evermore.

Psalm 122

¹ My heart was glad and filled with joy,
     my spirit danced and soared,
  When pilgrims said, *"Let's go and see
     the temple of the Lord."*

² And so it is that I embarked
     to journey far with them;
  And now our feet are by the gates
     that guard Jerusalem.

³ Jerusalem is beautiful,
     a city all can see;
  It's closely spaced and orderly,
     in splendid harmony.

⁴ It's here the tribes of Israel
     will thank the Lord with praise;
  For them this is an ordinance
     to follow all their days.

⁵ It's here the seats of justice rule
     and thrones of judgment shine;
  It's here the righteous come to find
     the thrones of David's line.

⁶ So pray this for Jerusalem
     so she will be at peace,
  *"May those who love her prosper much
     and have their worries cease.*

⁷ And may there be tranquility
and calm within her walls,
And safety and prosperity
throughout her palace halls."

⁸ O for the sake of those I love
and all that's good and true,
I say this to Jerusalem,
"may peace abide with you."

⁹ And for the temple of the Lord
and love that I profess,
I'll seek this for Jerusalem –
well-being and success.

Psalm 123

¹ O Lord, I lift my eyes to You,
I lift them to the sky;
I look to heaven where You dwell
and sit enthroned on high.

² Like slaves look to the master's hand
and maids their mistress' face,
We look to You, O Lord our God,
to bless us by Your grace.

³ O Lord, have mercy on our souls,
have mercy on us Lord;
For we are treated with contempt
and thoroughly abhorred.

⁴ Our souls are filled by mocking words
from those without a care,
And from the proud and arrogant
who leave us in despair.

Psalm 124

1 If God had not been on our side,
    would we say all was well?
What if the Lord had stayed away,
    what say you, Israel?

2 If God had not been on our side
    when we fought back the horde,
What would have been the consequence
    with no help from the Lord?

3 O surely when our foes attacked
    to crush us by their might,
They would have struck us in their rage
    and beat us in the fight.

4 For like the waters of a flood
    where people sink and drown,
They would have overwhelmed our lives
    until they pulled us down.

5 Or like a river running wild
    that swells and overflows,
They would have swept our souls away
    as raging waters rose.

6 So praise be to the Lord our God
    Who sees us here beneath;
He has not let our enemies
    attack us with their teeth.

7 Our soul is like a bird that flies
    escaping from the snare;
Because the snare has been destroyed,
    no more do we despair.

8 Our help comes from the Lord Most High,
    the One of greatest worth,
Who fashioned heaven high above,
    Creator of the earth.

Psalm 125

1 All those who put their trust in God
    and hope upon the Lord,
Are like Mount Zion's lofty peaks,
    which ever have endured.

2 For just as hills and mountaintops
    surround Jerusalem,
The Lord surrounds His chosen ones,
    forever watching them.

3 He'll stop the rod of wickedness
    from resting on their lands,
To keep the righteous from the urge
    of sinning with their hands.

4 O Lord, do good to those who act
    with virtue in their heart,
And those whose love and righteousness
    have set their lives apart.

5 But when You strike the wicked, Lord,
    strike those who stray as well;
And let tranquility and peace
    descend on Israel.

Psalm 126

1 The Lord brought us to Zion's peaks
    from exile far away;
It seemed like we were in a dream
    when we beheld that day.

2 Our tongues rang out with joyful songs,
    our laughter rose like doves;
The nations said, *"The Lord has done
    great things for those He loves."*

3 Indeed, the Lord has done great things
    to show His love and care;
  Our hearts are filled with happiness
    and joy beyond compare.

4 O Lord, restore our hopes again,
    our fortunes and our lands;
  And make us like a mighty stream
    that flows through desert sands.

5 For those who sow with tears of grief
    will reap a great delight,
  With joyful songs of happiness
    that let their hearts take flight.

6 Yes, those who weep when they go out
    while bearing seed to sow,
  Shall come again with shouts of joy
    with harvest sheaves aglow.

Psalm 127

1 Unless the Lord constructs the house,
    the builders only strain;
  Unless the Lord protects the town,
    the sentries guard in vain.

2 In vain one rises at the dawn
    and works till night for bread;
  For God provides for those He loves
    while they're asleep in bed.

3 O sons and daughters are from God –
    a blessing from the Lord;
  All children are a legacy –
    a real and just reward.

4 Like arrows in the archer's hand
    before the bow is strung,
  Are children who are born and thrive
    while parents still are young.

⁵ So happy those with quivers full
    for shame won't be their fate;
For they can face their enemies
    when near the city gate.

Psalm 128

¹ How happy those who fear the Lord
    and seek Him all their days,
And those who follow His commands
    by walking in His ways.

² For you will eat the food you grow,
    the labor of your hands;
And you will know prosperity,
    the harvest from your lands.

³ And your beloved wife will be
    much like a fruitful vine;
Your children stout like olive shoots
    that cluster where you dine.

⁴ By this your life is surely blessed,
    for this is your reward,
When you obey and follow God
    and always fear the Lord.

⁵ From Zion may the Lord bestow
    His blessings that ensure,
That you will see Jerusalem
    successful and secure.

⁶ And may you live to look upon
    grandchildren where you dwell;
So with these blessings raise a prayer
    of peace for Israel.

Psalm 129

¹ Let Israel repeat these words –
"O I have been oppressed;
The wicked have afflicted me
and put me to the test.

² *Yes, from my youth I've been oppressed*
by many enemies;
But they have not achieved success
or any victories.

³ *They wounded me by cutting deep*
like farmers till the dirt;
They sunk their plows into my back
and made each furrow hurt.

⁴ *But yet the Lord is good and just*
and watches over me;
He cut the cords of wickedness
to set this captive free."

⁵ O may those hating Zion fail
and turn back in defeat;
May they be shamed for what they've done
and forced into retreat.

⁶ May they be like the grass on roofs
where hot and dry winds blow,
Which withers in the noonday heat
before it starts to grow.

⁷ May there not be enough of it
to fill the reaper's hands,
Not sheaves to bind and take away,
nor single stalk that stands.

⁸ May none who pass the wicked say,
"O may the Lord bless you;
O let us bless you in His name
for all the things you do."

Psalm 130

1 O from the depths of my despair
   where all is dark and grey,
From suffering and hopelessness,
   O Lord, to You I pray.

2 O hear my voice call out to You,
   attend me in this place;
Please listen to my plaintive cry
   for mercy and Your grace.

3 If You recorded all our wrongs,
   our sins both great and small,
Could anyone be justified,
   could any stand at all?

4 But You extend forgiveness, Lord,
   despite what we are due;
And this is why we stand in awe
   and why we worship You.

5 I wait with patience for the Lord
   with hope that fills my soul;
I put my trust upon His word
   that it will make me whole.

6 O yes, my soul awaits the Lord
   like sentries seek the dawn;
Yet more than sentries search for light,
   my soul to God is drawn.

7 Let Israel now trust the Lord
   to save them from above;
Because He has abundant grace
   and never-failing love.

8 And He will rescue Israel
   from their iniquity;
The Lord Himself will ransom them
   to lift and set them free.

Psalm 131

1 O Lord, I've turned from arrogance
  and given up my pride;
 I do not ponder weighty things,
  I've put great thoughts aside.

2 For now my soul is like a child
  who's weaned and lays at rest;
 And like the child in mother's arms,
  my soul is truly blessed.

3 O Israel, believe the Lord
  and let your faith endure;
 O keep your hope and trust in Him
  both now and evermore.

Psalm 132

1 O Lord, remember David's plight,
  the wretchedness he knew;
 Recall his many troubles, Lord,
  the hardships suffered through.

2 O recollect the oath he swore
  about his holy quest;
 O Mighty God of Jacob, hear
  these words that he expressed:

3 *"I will not go into my house
  but live outside instead;
 I will not take a time to rest
  or lay upon my bed.*

4 *I will not stop or fall asleep
  or let my eyelids close;
 I will not slumber or recline
  or slow my pace to doze.*

⁵ *I will not pause until I find*
    a place the Lord can dwell,
  The God of Jacob, Mighty One,
    the God of Israel."

⁶ We heard his words in Ephrathah
    when near to Bethlehem;
  And on the plains and fields of Jaar
    we also learned of them.

⁷ And so we said, *"O let us go*
    to where the Lord is known;
  Let's worship in His dwelling place,
    the footstool of His throne."

⁸ O come into Your temple, Lord,
    and find Your resting place;
  And bring the symbol of Your might –
    the ark of strength and grace.

⁹ O may Your priests be clothed in robes
    of holy righteousness;
  And may Your saints sing praises, Lord,
    with joy and happiness.

¹⁰ And for the sake of David, Lord,
    who served You every day,
  Do not reject Your chosen one
    or turn Your face away.

¹¹ You spoke to David by Your word
    and made Your promise known:
  "O I will place a son of yours
    as king upon your throne.

¹² *And if his children follow me*
    by holding to my law,
  Then they'll forever keep the throne
    and govern over all."

¹³ O You have chosen Zion, Lord,
    to be where You will dwell;
For it is Your intended plan
    to live with Israel.

¹⁴ You tell us, *"Zion is my home*
    where I'll forever reign,
The site that I desire most,
    the heart of my domain.

¹⁵ *For those in Zion I will bless —*
    the hungry and the poor;
They'll eat until they've had their fill
    and do not want for more.

¹⁶ *I'll clothe her priests with victory*
    to set their spirits right;
And all her saints will sing for joy
    and shout with pure delight.

¹⁷ *It's here I'll strengthen David's line,*
    protected by my wing;
I'll set a lamp to be a light
    for my anointed king.

¹⁸ *I'll clothe his enemies with shame,*
    I'll crush and throw them down;
But he, the king, will reign supreme
    and wear a gleaming crown."

Psalm 133

¹ How wonderful and good to live
    in unity and peace,
To dwell in perfect harmony
    where joy and love increase.

² It's like the precious oil poured
    to cover Aaron's head,
That filled his beard and drenched his robe
    and soaked into each thread.

³ And it is like Mount Hermon's dew
   that rests on Zion's slope;
For there the Lord bestows His gift –
   eternal life and hope.

Psalm 134

¹ O praise the Lord you joyful souls,
   who serve Him with delight,
And you who stand within His house
   and watch throughout the night.

² And you within His temple courts,
   with hands and voices raised,
Exalt the Lord with all your heart
   and let His name be praised.

³ O may the Lord who made the earth
   and heaven high above,
Look down from Zion's holy hill
   and bless you with His love.

Psalm 135

¹ O praise the Lord and worship Him
   and glorify His name;
You servants of the Lord rejoice
   and celebrate His fame.

² Yes, you who stand inside His house
   and serve Him all your days,
From there within the courts of God,
   exalt His name in praise.

³ O praise the Lord and worship Him
   for He is good and right;
Sing praises to the name of God,
   for it is a delight.

⁴ The Lord chose Jacob and His seed
    to be for Him alone;
He called out those of Israel
    to treasure as His own.

⁵ The Lord is great, and does great things;
    He cannot be outdone;
He's greater than all other gods,
    exceeding everyone.

⁶ The Lord will do what pleases Him,
    whatever He decrees,
In heaven and upon the earth,
    and depths below the seas.

⁷ The Lord spreads clouds around the earth,
    He summons rain and storm;
He brings the wind from far away
    where gale and tempest form.

⁸ The Lord brought death to Egypt's heirs,
    His vengeance unrestrained;
He killed the firstborn child and beast
    so none of them remained.

⁹ But first He'd shown them many signs
    and wonders in their midst,
To punish Pharaoh and his court
    and those who would resist.

¹⁰ O many nations felt His wrath
    and power of His hand;
The Lord struck kings and princes down
    and wiped them from the land.

¹¹ King Og of Bashan was destroyed
    with kings of Canaanites,
As was the royal Sihon who
    had led the Amorites.

¹² The Lord made an inheritance
    from lands of those who fell;
  He gave it to the ones He loved,
    His people Israel.

¹³ O Lord, Your name is glorious
    and ever will endure;
  Throughout all generations, Lord,
    Your prominence is sure.

¹⁴ For You will give Your people hope
    and justice from above;
  You'll show them Your compassion, Lord,
    and wrap them in Your love.

¹⁵ The idols of the nations come
    from silver ore and gold;
  They are the work of human hands,
    created in a mold.

¹⁶ They have an open mouth but yet
    are silent as the night;
  They've eyes that stare out into space
    but don't have any sight.

¹⁷ They have two ears for listening
    but cannot hear a prayer;
  They have a mouth for drawing breath
    but cannot breathe the air.

¹⁸ Their makers will become like them,
    and thus will live their days,
  And so will those who trust in them
    and follow in their ways.

¹⁹ O Israel, now praise the Lord
    with loud and grateful voice;
  O house of Aaron, praise the Lord
    and let your heart rejoice.

²⁰ O house of Levi, praise the Lord
and glorify His name;
Let all who fear Him praise the Lord
with honor and acclaim.

²¹ O praise the Lord from Zion's gates,
O praise Him Israel;
Praise God within Jerusalem,
for there He's come to dwell.

Psalm 136

¹ O thank the Lord for He is good,
His righteousness is pure;
His love abides eternally,
enduring evermore.

² O thank the Lord, the God of gods,
that no one comes before;
His love abides eternally,
enduring evermore.

³ O thank the Lord, the Lord of lords,
to Whom our praises soar;
His love abides eternally,
enduring evermore.

⁴ O thank the Lord for miracles
that no one can ignore;
His love abides eternally,
enduring evermore.

⁵ O thank the Lord whose skill produced
the heavens we adore;
His love abides eternally,
enduring evermore.

⁶ O thank the Lord who built the earth
on seas that had no shore;
His love abides eternally,
enduring evermore.

7 O thank the Lord who placed the lights
    above to reassure;
  His love abides eternally,
    enduring evermore.

8 O thank the Lord for sun that rules
    by day so we're secure;
  His love abides eternally,
    enduring evermore.

9 O thank the Lord for moon and stars
    so night won't be obscure;
  His love abides eternally,
    enduring evermore.

10 O thank the Lord for striking down
    the first child Egypt bore;
  His love abides eternally,
    enduring evermore.

11 O thank the Lord for rescuing
    His people rich and poor;
  His love abides eternally,
    enduring evermore.

12 O thank the Lord who stretched His arm
    above the ocean's roar;
  His love abides eternally,
    enduring evermore.

13 O thank the Lord who touched the sea,
    which split as if it tore;
  His love abides eternally,
    enduring evermore.

14 O thank the Lord that Israel
    passed through and came ashore;
  His love abides eternally,
    enduring evermore.

¹⁵ O thank the Lord that Pharaoh drowned
  together with his corps;
 His love abides eternally,
  enduring evermore.

¹⁶ O thank the Lord who led the way
  across the desert floor;
 His love abides eternally,
  enduring evermore.

¹⁷ O thank the Lord who struck down kings
  and rulers by the score;
 His love abides eternally,
  enduring evermore.

¹⁸ O thank the Lord who slew great kings
  when on a field of war;
 His love abides eternally,
  enduring evermore.

¹⁹ O thank the Lord that Amorites
  saw Sihon not endure;
 His love abides eternally,
  enduring evermore.

²⁰ O thank the Lord that king Og's death
  made Bashan insecure;
 His love abides eternally,
  enduring evermore.

²¹ O thank the Lord who gave their land
  to those He would restore;
 His love abides eternally,
  enduring evermore.

²² O thank the Lord that Israel
  was well provided for;
 His love abides eternally,
  enduring evermore.

²³ O thank the Lord who gave us help
      when we were pressed and poor;
   His love abides eternally,
      enduring evermore.

²⁴ O thank the Lord who set us free
      from foes that we abhor;
   His love abides eternally,
      enduring evermore.

²⁵ O thank the Lord who gives us food
      from His abundant store;
   His love abides eternally,
      enduring evermore.

²⁶ O thank the Lord, our God who reigns
      in heaven where it's pure;
   His love abides eternally,
      enduring evermore.

Psalm 137

¹ By rivers near to Babylon,
      we settled down and wept,
   Recalling Zion in our hearts
      where memories are kept.

² And as we sat, our harps were hung
      upon the willow trees;
   No sound arose from idle strings
      to waft upon the breeze.

³ But then our captors made us sing
      despite our wretched plight;
   They said, *"Sing songs of Zion's days
      that fill us with delight."*

⁴ O how could we sing songs to them
      that once were for the Lord?
   How could we sing in foreign lands
      when we were not restored?

⁵ O hear my pledge, Jerusalem,
    to always think of you;
  If not, then may my right hand lose
    the skill that once it knew.

⁶ And may my tongue stick in my mouth
    if I forget your ways,
  Or if I fail, Jerusalem,
    to love you all my days.

⁷ O Lord, recall Jerusalem,
    the day when it came down,
  And how the Edomites cried out,
    "O crush it to the ground!"

⁸ O Babylon, your time is short,
    destruction is your fate;
  For happy are the ones who make
    you pay for all your hate.

⁹ Yes, it is well with those who act
    to punish what you've done,
  Like using rocks to strike the heads
    of every little one.

Psalm 138

¹ O Lord, I'll thank and honor You
    with heart and mind ablaze;
  Before the gods I'll give You thanks
    and offer songs of praise.

² I'll praise You in Your temple courts
    for faithfulness and love;
  For You have made Your word supreme
    and set Your name above.

³ You answered when I called to You,
    responding to my plea;
  You fortified my spirit, Lord,
    with hope that strengthened me.

⁴ May princes come from east and west,
    and kings from north and south,
To praise and thank You for each word
    that's spoken from Your mouth.

⁵ May they declare Your awesome deeds
    by singing of Your ways;
Because, O Lord, You're glorious,
    and worthy of all praise.

⁶ Although You are exalted, Lord,
    You hold the lowly dear,
But know the proud from far away
    and do not venture near.

⁷ And though I face adversity,
    still You preserve my soul;
Your right hand strikes my enemies
    to save and keep me whole.

⁸ O Lord, do all that You have planned
    to help me from above;
Don't spurn the work that You began
    by Your eternal love.

Psalm 139

¹ O Lord, You have examined me,
    discerning what's inside;
You know my every thought and deed,
    there's nothing I can hide.

² You know when I am sitting down,
    You know when I arise;
You know my thinking from afar,
    whatever I devise.

³ You know when I am going out,
    You know when I'm at rest;
You know the places I have been,
    You know my worst and best.

⁴ Before a word is on my tongue,
    You know what I will say;
  You know what I am thinking, Lord,
    the thoughts that I'll convey.

⁵ You're all around on every side,
    behind me and before;
  You lay Your hand upon my head
    so I can rest secure.

⁶ The things You know are wonderful,
    magnificent and grand;
  Such knowledge is too difficult
    for me to understand.

⁷ Is there a place that I can go
    where You won't follow me?
  Can I escape Your Spirit, Lord,
    or from Your presence flee?

⁸ If I climb to the heavens, Lord,
    upon the highest stair,
  Or if I plunge the lowest depths,
    I know that You are there.

⁹ If I should rise on wings of dawn
    to find a place to dwell,
  And settle down across the sea,
    I'll find You there as well.

¹⁰ For even there Your hand will guide
    and show me how to grow;
  And with Your right hand holding fast,
    You will not let me go.

¹¹ O I could say, *"I'll hide from You*
    when darkness fills the night,
  When all that shines has left the sky
    and blackness veils the light."

¹² But there's no darkness dark enough,
 no night where You can't see,
No blackness that's so black, O Lord,
 where You can't follow me.

¹³ O Lord, Your hand created me –
 my body and my soul;
You knit me in my mother's womb,
 You planned and made me whole.

¹⁴ I praise You for the way I'm formed,
 the wonder of it all;
Because Your works are marvelous,
 I stand in fear and awe.

¹⁵ You saw my bones as they were formed,
 and I was framed for birth,
As I was growing secretly
 within the depths of earth.

¹⁶ You saw my life before I breathed,
 and this was not by chance;
My days were written in Your book,
 You knew them in advance.

¹⁷ How precious are Your thoughts to me,
 how wonderful and great;
How large their number, no one knows,
 a sum no one can state.

¹⁸ For if my mind could count them, Lord,
 they'd be like grains of sand;
Yet waking from such pondering,
 I'd still be in Your hand.

¹⁹ O how I wish that You would strike
 and make the wicked flee;
O fly away you murderers,
 depart and run from me.

²⁰ O Lord, they mock You with their words
    that slander and defame;
Your enemies spew blasphemies
    and speak against Your name.

²¹ O how I hate those hating You
    and those who disobey;
For I am grieved when anyone
    rebels against Your way.

²² I loathe them so completely, Lord,
    my mind and body seize;
Because they stand against Your name,
    I count them enemies.

²³ Examine me with care, O Lord,
    and probe my heart anew;
Inspect my mind and search my thoughts
    and all the things I do.

²⁴ O see if I've been wicked, Lord,
    or if I've gone astray;
And lead me down Your perfect path
    and everlasting way.

Psalm 140

¹ O come now, Lord, and rescue me
    from all whose hearts are vile;
Preserve me from their violence,
    and guard me from their guile.

² Deliver me from all their schemes
    and evil You abhor;
For every day they stir up strife
    intent on making war.

³ Their tongues are as a serpent's fang
    that's sharpened like a stake;
The poison underneath their lips
    like venom of a snake.

⁴ O keep me from the wicked, Lord,
    and save me from their grip;
Preserve me from the violent
    who plot to make me trip.

⁵ The proud have set a trap for me,
    they've laid a hidden snare;
They spread a net along my way
    to catch me unaware.

⁶ O Lord, You are my only God,
    please listen to my plea –
My heartfelt cry for mercy, Lord,
    to pour Your grace on me.

⁷ Almighty Lord, Deliverer,
    my stronghold and my shield,
Protect my head throughout the fight
    so I will never yield.

⁸ Don't grant the wicked what they want
    or give them what they need;
For they will boast if their deceit
    and evil plans succeed.

⁹ But let the heads of those who come
    to threaten and condemn,
Have all the mischief of their lips
    fall down and cover them.

¹⁰ O let them burn from red-hot coals
    that rain down from the skies;
Then throw them in a miry pit
    from which they'll never rise.

¹¹ May slanderers not settle down
    or find a place to rest;
And those consumed with violence
    be thoroughly oppressed.

12 O Lord, I know that You uphold
 the causes of the poor;
So justice comes to those in need
 to make their lives secure.

13 And thus the righteous will give thanks
 and lift Your name in praise,
Abiding in Your presence, Lord,
 encompassed by Your gaze.

Psalm 141

1 O Lord, I'm desperate for Your help
 so listen to my cry;
Please hear me when I call to You
 and hasten Your reply.

2 Receive my prayer as incense, Lord,
 infusing like a spice,
My lifted hands an offering –
 the evening sacrifice.

3 Lord, post a guard around my mouth
 to watch my every word,
A sentinel to mind my lips
 before my tongue is stirred.

4 O keep my heart from evil thoughts
 and acting out in sin;
Don't let the treats the wicked eat
 attract and draw me in.

5 A righteous blow I'll not refuse,
 it's oil on my head;
But actions born of wickedness
 I'll pray against instead.

6 O may the wicked see their kings
 be dashed on rocky ground,
So they will know the words I spoke
 were accurate and sound.

⁷ For like the earth is broken up
    by plows that till the land,
Their bones lie shattered near the grave
    and scattered in the sand.

⁸ O Lord, my eyes are fixed on You,
    in You I place my trust;
So do not let my soul taste death
    or turn me back to dust.

⁹ But shelter and deliver me
    from every trap and snare;
Don't let an evil net that's spread
    surprise me unaware.

¹⁰ O let the wicked trip and fall
    into the traps they set;
And guide me, Lord, around their nets
    so they are not a threat.

Psalm 142

¹ O Lord, I cry aloud to You
    to listen to my plea;
I lift my voice for mercy, Lord,
    that You would answer me.

² I come to You with my complaints
    of how I am oppressed;
I tell You of the miseries
    that leave my soul distressed.

³ O when I'm faint in spirit, Lord,
    You watch me on my way;
For on my path are hidden snares
    the wicked set each day.

⁴ You know that I am all alone,
    I've none who will console;
I have no friend who watches me
    or cares about my soul.

5 And so, O Lord, I cry to You
   when I am facing strife;
   For You're my refuge and my strength,
   my portion in this life.

6 Defend me when You hear my cry
   for urgent is my need;
   My enemies are far too strong
   and break me like a reed.

7 O free my soul from prison, Lord,
   and I will sing Your praise;
   The righteous then will gather round
   for gracious are Your ways.

Psalm 143

1 O Lord, please listen to my prayer
   for I am filled with grief;
   In faithfulness and righteousness,
   draw near for my relief.

2 O do not judge my wayward soul
   although this is Your right;
   For there is no one who is pure
   or righteous in Your sight.

3 My foes pursue and tear at me
   till I am crushed and ripped;
   They make me live where all is dark
   like deep within a crypt.

4 My spirit is despondent, Lord,
   beyond what I can bear;
   My heart within me is appalled,
   dismayed and in despair.

5 Yet I recall Your ancient deeds,
   Your marvels in the lands;
   I meditate upon Your works
   and wonders of Your hands.

⁶ I open up my arms to You
  and reach them to the sky;
For I am thirsting for You, Lord,
  like land that's parched and dry.

⁷ Come quickly, Lord, and answer me,
  my spirit's growing weak;
Don't hide from me or I will fall
  into a pit that's bleak.

⁸ But let the dawn tell of Your love
  because I trust in You;
I pray that You would guide my way
  and teach me what to do.

⁹ O save me from my enemies,
  and keep me from their sword;
For You are my security,
  my strength and refuge, Lord.

¹⁰ Because You are my one true God,
  instruct me in Your will;
And let Your Spirit lead the way
  to level every hill.

¹¹ And for the glory of Your name,
  revive and rescue me;
Preserve me by Your righteousness,
  and end my misery.

¹² O by Your everlasting grace
  extinguish every foe;
Because I am Your servant, Lord,
  destroy them with a blow.

Psalm 144

¹ O praises to the Lord my Rock
  Who strengthens by His might;
He trains my hands to go to war,
  my fingers for the fight.

² The Lord is my protecting shield
    Who loves and watches me,
My stronghold and deliverer
    Who gives the victory.

³ O who are we that You should care
    or think about us, Lord,
That we are looked upon by You
    and simply not ignored?

⁴ For we are like a fleeting breath,
    a shadow in the haze,
Like vapor in a swirling wind
    that sweeps away our days.

⁵ O open up the heavens, Lord,
    and hasten to come down;
Then touch the mountains with Your hand
    till smoke pours from the ground.

⁶ Cast down Your lighting from the sky
    to rout the enemy;
Shoot flaming arrows at my foes
    until they turn and flee.

⁷ Deliver me from high above
    when waters flood the lands;
Protect me from the foreigners
    who'd strike me with their hands.

⁸ Preserve my soul from those whose tongues
    speak only with deceit,
And those whose right hands are not true,
    but always lie and cheat.

⁹ Then I will sing a song to You,
    a song that's fresh and new;
I'll play it on the ten-stringed harp
    to praise and worship You.

¹⁰ For You give kings the victory,
  it comes from You, O Lord;
You saved Your servant David's life
  and kept him from the sword.

¹¹ So shield me from the foreigners
  whose tongues are full of lies,
Who clutch deceit in their right hands
  and hold it in disguise.

¹² O may our sons be straight and true
  like branches on a vine,
Our daughters like the polished stones
  that make a palace shine.

¹³ May all our barns be filled with food
  from bumper harvest yields;
May there be tens of thousands sheep
  that graze upon our fields.

¹⁴ May all our oxen labor strong,
  may no one break our wall;
May no cries sound within our streets
  and no disaster fall.

¹⁵ How happy those who have these things,
  for such is their reward;
How happy those whose only God
  is He who is the Lord.

Psalm 145

¹ O God, I'll always honor You,
  exalting You as King;
And I will ever bless Your name
  with praises that I sing.

² My soul will bless and worship You
  both now and all my days;
My lips will glorify Your name
  and ever sing Your praise.

³ For You are great and worthy, Lord,
and praised by those below;
Your greatness is beyond compare,
much more than we can know.

⁴ Each generation will proclaim
to others in the land,
The wonder of Your mighty acts
and marvels from Your hand.

⁵ They'll celebrate Your majesty,
so glorious and great;
And I will think about Your works
and on them meditate.

⁶ They'll speak about Your awesome deeds
and power of the same;
And I will tell how great You are,
Your wonders I'll proclaim.

⁷ They'll recollect Your goodness, Lord,
the many ways You bless;
With gladness in their hearts they'll sing
about Your righteousness.

⁸ O Lord, You're kind and merciful
and quick with Your embrace;
You're slow to anger and rebuke
and full of love and grace.

⁹ Yes, You are good to everyone
despite how far they've strayed;
You have compassion and concern
for all whom You have made.

¹⁰ So those whom You've created, Lord,
will praise and worship You;
And all Your saints will give Your name
the honor that it's due.

¹¹ They'll speak of how Your kingdom shines
    and of its majesty;
    They'll talk about Your awesome strength
    and power all can see.

¹² They'll tell the world about Your deeds
    and breadth of Your domain,
    Your kingdom and its majesty,
    the splendor of Your reign.

¹³ Your kingdom is forever, Lord,
    and always will endure;
    You're faithful to Your promises,
    and all Your works are pure.

¹⁴ You care for those who need Your help
    and hold them when they fall;
    You raise the broken and distressed
    so they can stand up tall.

¹⁵ All living things have fixed their gaze
    to keep You in their sight;
    And You provide them food to eat
    to sate their appetite.

¹⁶ For You have opened wide Your hand
    and let Your blessings flow;
    You give us our desires, Lord
    to fill us here below.

¹⁷ The Lord is righteous in His ways,
    and just how He proceeds;
    He's merciful in every act
    and kind in all His deeds.

¹⁸ The Lord is close to those who pray,
    from them He won't depart;
    He knows of their sincerity,
    the candor of their heart.

¹⁹ The Lord fulfills the needs of those
   who hold His name in awe;
   He listens when they lift their cries,
   He saves them when they call.

²⁰ The Lord protects those loving Him,
   whose hearts are overjoyed;
   But those who act in wickedness
   will surely be destroyed.

²¹ So I will sing unto the Lord
   with praises to His name;
   Let every creature here below
   forever do the same.

Psalm 146

¹ Sing hallelujah to the Lord,
   His majesty proclaim;
   O come, my soul, and praise the Lord
   and glorify His name.

² I'll worship God with every breath
   and ever sing His praise;
   Yes, I will always honor Him
   with praises all my days.

³ O do not trust in prince or king
   to keep you from the grave;
   Don't put your hope in human hands
   whose power cannot save.

⁴ For when they take their final breath,
   their bodies turn to dust;
   Their thoughts and plans will die with them
   with nothing left to trust.

⁵ But happy those who place their faith
   and hope upon the Lord,
   And those the God of Jacob helps
   for they'll be reassured.

⁶ For God made heaven, earth, and sea
   and all that they contain;
His faithfulness has long endured
   and ever will remain.

⁷ The Lord shows justice to the poor
   and those too weak to see;
The Lord provides the hungry food
   and sets the captives free.

⁸ The Lord lifts those who've fallen down
   and gives the blind their sight;
He loves the godly and their ways
   because they do what's right.

⁹ The Lord consoles the orphaned child
   and widow all their days;
The Lord helps strangers, but rebukes
   the wicked for their ways.

¹⁰ The Lord God reigns eternally,
   let Zion thus proclaim;
So generations throughout time
   will ever praise His name.

Psalm 147

¹ How good it is to praise the Lord,
   how pleasant to rejoice;
How right it is to worship Him
   and thank Him with our voice.

² The Lord restores Jerusalem
   so once again it stands;
He calls the lost of Israel
   to come from distant lands.

³ He heals the broken-hearted soul,
   the downcast and alone;
He binds their wounds with tender care,
   restoring flesh and bone.

⁴ The Lord has counted every star,
    each one a burning flame;
  For He has placed them in the sky
    and calls each one by name.

⁵ The Lord is great and powerful,
    and awesome is His might;
  His understanding's infinite,
    and perfect is His sight.

⁶ The Lord lifts up the mild and meek
    and frees the soul that's bound,
  But breaks the wicked for their ways
    and throws them to the ground.

⁷ So thank the Lord and worship Him
    with every voice that sings;
  And play the sweetest melody
    on harp of many strings.

⁸ The Lord spreads clouds across the sky
    so earth receives its rain;
  He makes the grass grow thick and green
    on every hill and plain.

⁹ The Lord provides for animals
    within each field and stall;
  He gives the ravens food to eat
    whenever one should call.

¹⁰ The Lord does not enjoy a horse
    despite its strength and might;
  Nor does He find in human legs
    a reason to delight.

¹¹ But rather He is pleased with those
    who trust Him in their hearts,
  Who hope in His unfailing love
    and mercy He imparts.

¹² O praise the Lord, Jerusalem,
  and glorify His name;
 Yes, Zion come and praise Your God,
  His honor to proclaim.

¹³ The Lord ensures your gates are strong
  and guards your boundaries;
 He blesses all the youth within
  to put their souls at ease.

¹⁴ The Lord endows your land with peace
  and keeps you from defeat;
 He satisfies your hunger pains
  with finest grains of wheat.

¹⁵ The Lord sends His commandments out
  to everyone on earth;
 His word runs swiftly through the lands
  so all will know its worth.

¹⁶ The Lord spreads snow that sprinkles down
  like wool at shearing time;
 He scatters frost that sparkles white
  like crumbled ash and lime.

¹⁷ The Lord makes hail erupt from clouds
  like pebbles being thrown.
 O who can stand the icy cold
  and power He has shown?

¹⁸ The Lord then speaks a single word
  that melts the ice below;
 He slowly breathes, the breezes stir,
  and waters start to flow.

¹⁹ The Lord reveals His just decrees
  so Jacob knows His ways;
 He gives his law to Israel
  to follow all their days.

[20] The Lord has not disclosed these things
  to those He does not love,
But only gives them to His own,
  so praise the Lord above.

Psalm 148

[1] O praise the Lord and worship Him,
  sing praises from the sky;
From heaven praise and honor Him,
  O praise Him from on high.

[2] O praise the Lord, angelic ones,
  come join and sing His praise;
O praise Him, all you royal host,
  exalt Him all your days.

[3] O praise the Lord, you sun and moon,
  just praise Him where you are;
O praise the Lord, you astral lights,
  each bright and shining star.

[4] O praise the Lord, you mighty realm
  of heaven from on high;
O praise the Lord, you waters formed
  beyond the earth and sky.

[5] O praise the Lord, all things above,
  and glorify His name;
For His command created you
  so give Him your acclaim.

[6] O praise the Lord, all things on high,
  He's fixed you in your place,
Where He decreed you'd ever stay
  forever by His grace.

[7] O praise the Lord and worship Him,
  you here on earth below;
O praise Him creatures of the deep
  where currents ebb and flow.

⁸ O praise the Lord, you elements
    of lightning, snow and hail,
And every wind at His command
    that rises to a gale.

⁹ O praise the Lord, you mountain tops,
    and hills above the seas,
And mighty cedars standing tall,
    and verdant orchard trees.

¹⁰ O praise the Lord, you animals,
    who live in field and stall,
And every bird that takes to wing,
    all creatures great and small.

¹¹ O praise the Lord, you mighty kings
    and princes of the earth,
And every sovereign governor
    of high and noble birth.

¹² O praise the Lord, all you who breathe,
    both young and very old,
You men and women, children too,
    and multitudes untold.

¹³ O praise the Lord, created things,
    exalt His name on high;
His glory is above the earth,
    the heavens and the sky.

¹⁴ O praise the Lord for He gives strength
    to those that He's restored;
So Israel and those He loves
    come praise Him, praise the Lord.

Psalm 149

¹ O praise the Lord and worship Him
    with honor and acclaim;
O sing a new song to the Lord
    with those who love His name.

2 Let Israel rejoice in Him,
   their Maker and their King;
Let Zion shout with thankfulness
   as joyfully they sing.

3 O praise the Lord with song and dance,
   and make a joyful scene;
Play music to the Lord with harp
   and on the tambourine.

4 The Lord takes joy in those He loves,
   in them He finds delight;
He gives the humble victory
   and saves them by His might.

5 So let the saints be filled with joy
   to think of what He's done;
O let them sing upon their beds
   before the day's begun.

6 And let their voices shout aloud
   with praises to the Lord;
While tightly in their hands they hold
   and wield a two-edged sword.

7 Their sword will mete out punishment
   to nations all around;
The wicked will be disciplined
   by blades that strike them down.

8 The heathen kings will be subdued,
   then tightly bound and chained,
Their nobles clasped by iron bands
   so they will be restrained.

9 By God's command this punishment
   will be their just reward;
And thus, God's people will prevail,
   so praise Him, praise the Lord.

Psalm 150

1 O praise the Lord and worship Him
  within the temple hall;
  O praise Him where He dwells on high
  and where He's held in awe.

2 O praise the Lord for all His deeds
  of power and of worth;
  O praise Him that He's unsurpassed
  in heaven and the earth.

3 O praise the Lord with trumpet blast
  and sound a mighty strain;
  O praise Him with a lyre's tune
  to echo a refrain.

4 O praise the Lord with ten-stringed harp
  and music of the lute;
  O praise Him with the tambourine
  and on the pipe and flute.

5 O praise the Lord with cymbal notes
  resounding as they ring;
  O praise Him with repeating chords
  and harmony they bring.

6 Let everything that draws a breath
  arise with one accord,
  And sing with joyful voices raised
  to praise Him, praise the Lord.

www.ingramcontent.com/pod-product-compliance
Lightning Source LLC
La Vergne TN
LVHW051223080426
835513LV00016B/1386